BiBLe PUZZLES FOR BOYS

Ty Van Hofstetter

SUPER BIBLE PUZZLES FOR BOYS

SHILOH kidz
An Imprint of Barbour Publishing, Inc.

© 2014 by Barbour Publishing, Inc.

ISBN 978-1-68322-988-9

All rights reserved. No part of this publication may be reproduced or transmitted for commercial purposes, except for brief quotations in printed reviews, without written permission of the publisher.

Churches and other noncommercial interests may reproduce portions of this book without the express written permission of Barbour Publishing, provided that the text does not exceed 500 words or 5 percent of the entire book, whichever is less, and that the text is not material quoted from another publisher. When reproducing text from this book, include the following credit line: "From *Super Bible Puzzles for Boys*, published by Barbour Publishing, Inc. Used by permission."

All Scripture quotations are from the King James Version of the Bible.

Published by Shiloh Kidz, an imprint of Barbour Publishing, 1810 Barbour Drive, Uhrichsville, Ohio 44683, www.shilohkidz.com

Our mission is to inspire the world with the life-changing message of the Bible.

Printed in the United States of America.
006541 0519   BP

Contents

Introduction 9

1. Creation 10
2. Adam Created 12
3. Planet-Wide Flooding 14
4. The Raven and the Dove 16
5. The Tower of Babel 18
6. Two Cities Completely Destroyed 20
7. An Almost-Sacrifice 22
8. The Stolen Blessing 24
9. Wrestle Mania 26
10. Betrayed 28
11. Moses' Calling 30
12. Passed Over 32
13. Parting of the Red Sea 34
14. The Ten Commandments 36
15. The Golden Calf 38
16. Consequences of Poor Choices 40
17. The Brass Serpent 42
18. Super-Strong City Walls Crumble to Dust .. 44
19. Treaty with Deceivers 46

20. The Day the Sun Did Not Move 48
21. 300 Men (and the Lord) vs. a Huge Army 50
22. A Hairy Situation 52
23. Idol Mysteriously Bows
    Before the Lord's Ark 54
24. Goliath! 56
25. David and Goliath 58
26. David and Saul 60
27. King Saul's Creepy Night 62
28. Absalom 64
29. A Young King Asks for Wisdom 66
30. Daily Fed by Birds 68
31. True God vs. False God 70
32. Chariot of Fire 72
33. The Floating Axe 74
34. A King Shows Off for Foreigners 76
35. No Earthly Protection 78
36. Nehemiah and the Bullies 80
37. I'm a Sheep! 82
38. A Test without Royal Food 84
39. Mysterious Writing on a Wall 86
40. The Big Cats 88
41. Big Fish Swallows Little Guy 90

42. A Mute Lesson 92

43. Baby Jesus' First Visitors 94

44. An Old Man and a Baby 96

45. More Visitors for Young Jesus 98

46. Jesus Calls His First Disciples 100

47. Jesus' First Miracle 102

48. Rock vs. Sand 104

49. Sick Servant Miraculously Healed 106

50. Dinner with Sinners 108

51. The Dragnet 110

52. Walking on Water 112

53. Friends Help a Man Find Healing 114

54. The Four Soils 116

55. The Great Storm 118

56. Demons Leave a Man to Enter Pigs 120

57. Mountaintop Transfiguration 122

58. Children and the Kingdom of God 124

59. Who Can Be Saved? 126

60. The Good Neighbor 128

61. A Foolish Man 130

62. A Prodigal ("Wasteful") Man 132

63. Parable of a Rich Man and a Poor Man 134

64. One Thankful and Nine Forgetful Lepers 136

65. Zacchaeus 138
66. Born Twice 140
67. Feeding the 5,000 142
68. A Blind Man Sees 144
69. Jesus Raises a Friend from the Dead 146
70. A Powerful Example 148
71. Jesus Comforts His Troubled Disciples 150
72. Palm Sunday 152
73. The Lord's Supper 154
74. Garden of Gethsemane 156
75. Hearing Problems 158
76. A Rooster Crows 160
77. Barabbas Gets Freedom—
    Jesus Gets Death 162
78. Jesus Killed! 164
79. Jesus Buried 166
80. Resurrection! 168
81. Thomas Doubts 170
82. Ascension 172
83. The Birth of the Church 174
84. Mighty Jesus 176
Answers 178

WELCOME TO SUPER BIBLE PUZZLES FOR BOYS!

The Bible is jam-packed with exciting stories—from the creation of Adam to the parting of the Red Sea, from the battle for Jericho to Jesus' ascension into heaven. In the pages to follow, you'll find dozens of word search and crossword puzzles to test your knowledge of each story!

Super Bible Puzzles for Boys provides hours of good, clean fun. Best of all, you'll be learning more and more about God's Word, the Bible. What could be better than that?

All Bible quotations are taken from the classic King James Version of scripture—and all answers will be in the King James spelling. Multiple words underlined side by side in the word search scriptures will be found together in the puzzle. Other single search words will appear in bold. Have a Bible (or a Bible website) handy when you solve the puzzles. . .that's okay, it's not cheating! The whole idea is to get you deeper into God's Word.

For added fun, you'll find some amazing trivia questions sprinkled throughout. Puzzle answers begin on page 178, while the trivia answers are set upside down below each question.

Have fun!

1. CREATION
GENESIS 1:1-31

ACROSS

5. What God did "in the beginning" (v. 1)

6. What else did God create besides male? (v. 27)

8. One of the things man is to "have dominion" (rule) over (v. 26)

9. The lights in the firmament (sky) are to mark years and what else? (v. 14)

DOWN

1. The day God called the firmament Heaven (sky) (v. 8)

2. Who created the heaven and the earth? (v. 1)

3. What else did God create besides female (v. 27)

4. God created man using His what as an example? (v. 26)

6. The day God created "Day" and "Night" (v. 5)

7. Another name for "Earth" (v. 10)

2. ADAM CREATED
GENESIS 2:7-8

And the LORD God **formed man** of the **dust** of the **ground**, and breathed into his **nostrils** the **breath** of **life**; and man became a living soul. And the LORD God **planted** a **garden** eastward in **Eden**; and **there** he **put** the man whom he had formed.

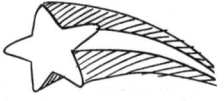 **BONUS TRIVIA!**

How did Jacob describe his brother Esau?
- a) scary
- b) wary
- c) hairy
- d) merry

Answer: c) hairy (Genesis 27:11)

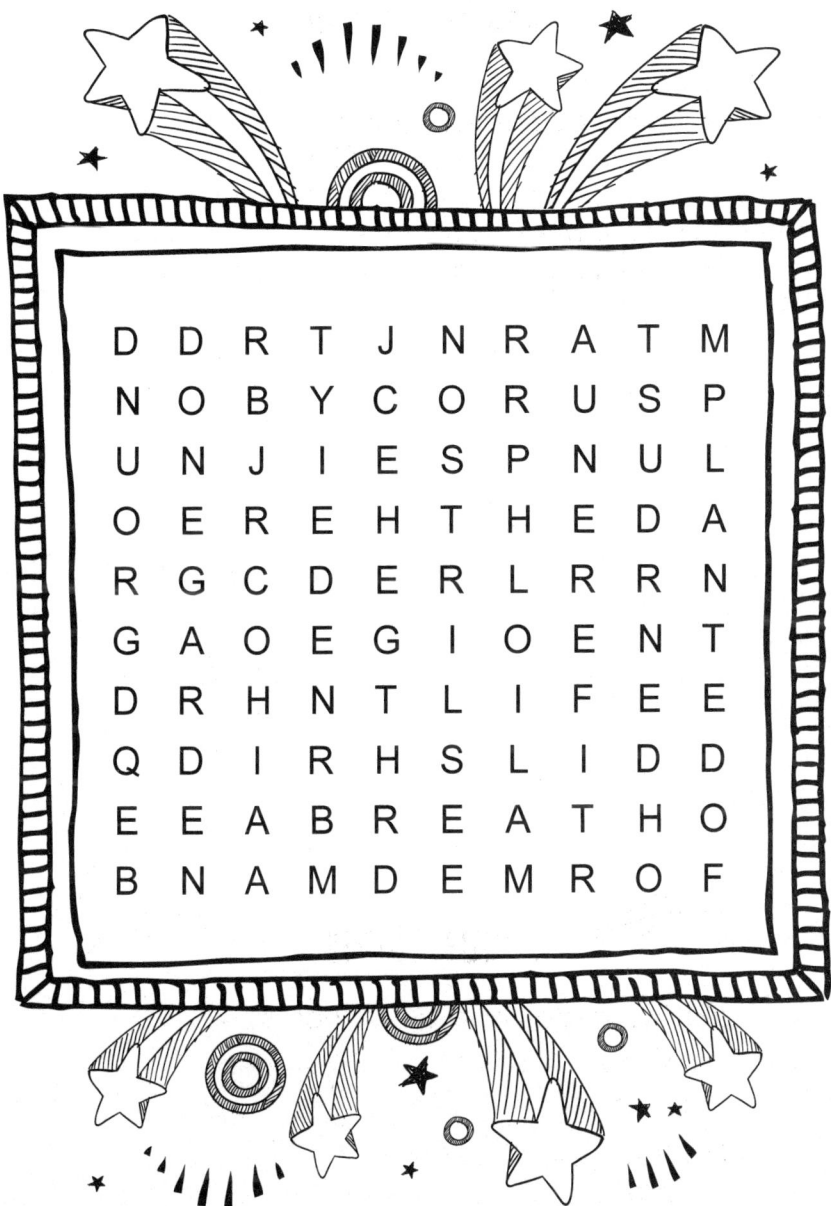

3. PLANET-WIDE FLOODING
GENESIS 7:17-24

And the **flood** was **forty** days upon the earth; and the waters **increased**, and bare up the ark, and it was lift up above the earth. And the waters prevailed, and were increased greatly upon the earth; and the **ark** went upon the face of the waters. And the waters prevailed exceedingly upon the earth; and all the high **hills**, that were under the whole heaven, were **covered**. Fifteen cubits upward did the waters prevail; and the mountains were covered. And all flesh **died** that moved upon the earth, both of fowl, and of cattle, and of beast, and of every creeping thing that creepeth upon the earth, and every man: All in whose nostrils was the **breath** of life, of all that was in the **dry** land, died. And every living substance was destroyed which was upon the face of the ground, both man, and cattle, and the creeping things, and the fowl of the heaven; and they were destroyed from the earth: and **Noah** only remained **alive**, and they that were with him in the ark. And the waters prevailed upon the **earth** an hundred and fifty days.

4. THE RAVEN AND THE DOVE
GENESIS 8:6-12

And it came to pass at the end of forty days, that Noah **opened** the **window** of the **ark** which he had made: And he sent forth a **raven**, which went forth to and fro, until the **waters** were dried up from off the earth. Also he sent forth a dove from him, to see if the waters were abated from off the face of the ground; But the **dove** found no rest for the sole of her foot, and she returned unto him into the ark, for the waters were on the face of the whole earth: then he put forth his **hand**, and took her, and pulled her in unto him into the ark. And he stayed yet other **seven** days; and **again** he sent forth the dove out of the ark; And the dove came in to him in the **evening**; and, lo, in her mouth was an <u>olive leaf</u> pluckt off: so Noah **knew** that the waters were abated from off the earth. And he stayed yet other seven days; and sent forth the dove; which returned not again unto him any more.

5. The Tower of Babel
GENESIS 11:1–9

And the whole earth was of one language, and of one speech. And it came to pass, as they journeyed from the east, that they found a plain in the land of **Shinar**; and they dwelt there. And they said one to another, Go to, let us make **brick**, and burn them thoroughly. And they had brick for stone, and slime had they for morter. And they said, Go to, let us **build** us a city and a **tower**, whose top may **reach** unto heaven; and let us make us a name, lest we be scattered abroad upon the face of the whole earth. And the Lord came **down** to see the city and the tower, which the children of men builded. And the Lord said, Behold, the people is one, and they have all **one** language; and this they begin to do: and now nothing will be restrained from them, which they have imagined to do. Go to, let us go down, and there confound their language, that they may not understand one another's speech. So the Lord **scattered** them abroad from thence upon the face of all the earth: and they left off to build the **city**. Therefore is the **name** of it called **Babel**; because the Lord did there confound the language of all the earth: and from thence did the Lord scatter them abroad upon the face of all the **earth**.

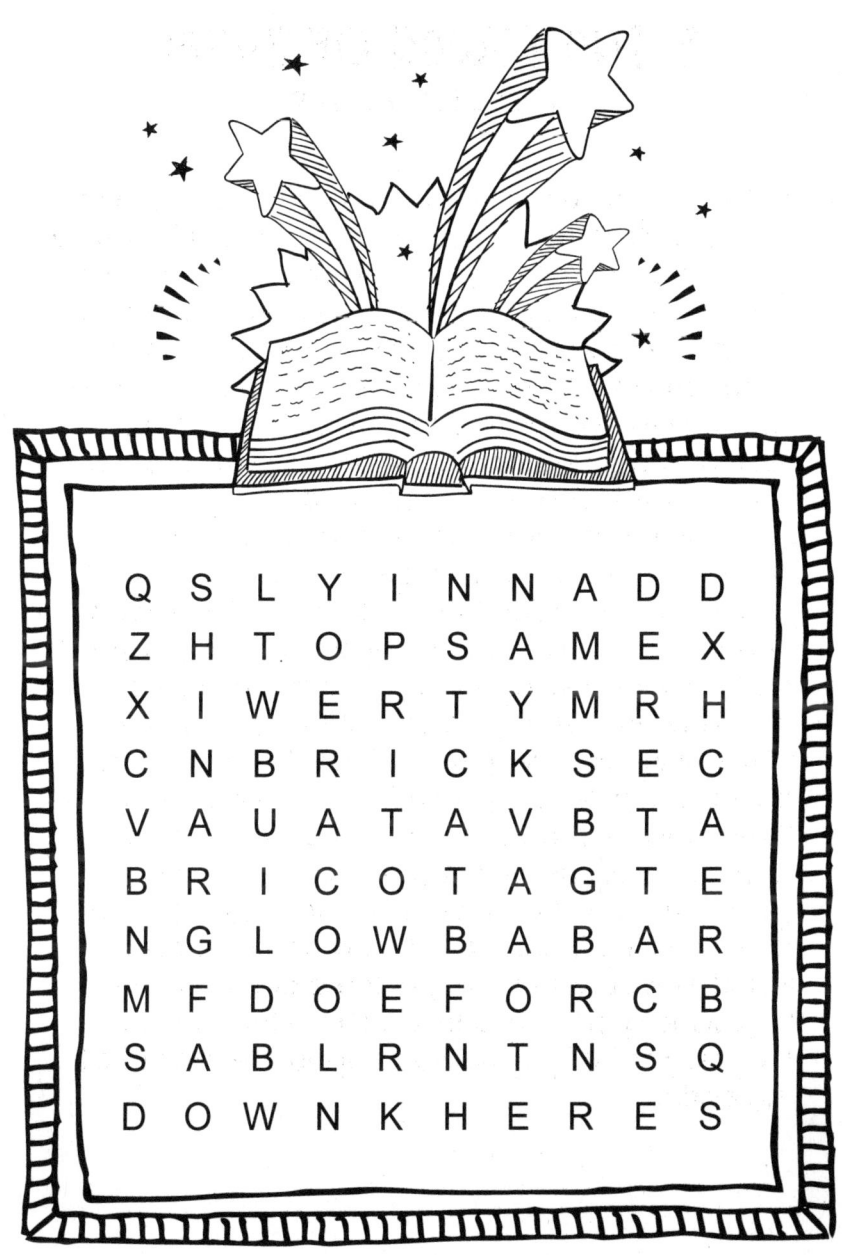

6. Two Cities Completely Destroyed
GENESIS 19:15–30

ACROSS

1. What the mysterious men took hold of on Lot and his family (v. 16)
5. One of the two cities the Lord destroyed (v. 24)
6. Lot's wife became a pillar of this (v. 26)
8. Abraham saw this where the two cities used to be (v. 28)

DOWN

2. They told Lot to hurry and make his family run away (v. 15)
3. The name of the city Lot wanted to go to (v. 22)
4. The place where Lot and his two daughters went (v. 30)
7. The family member who looked back (v. 26)

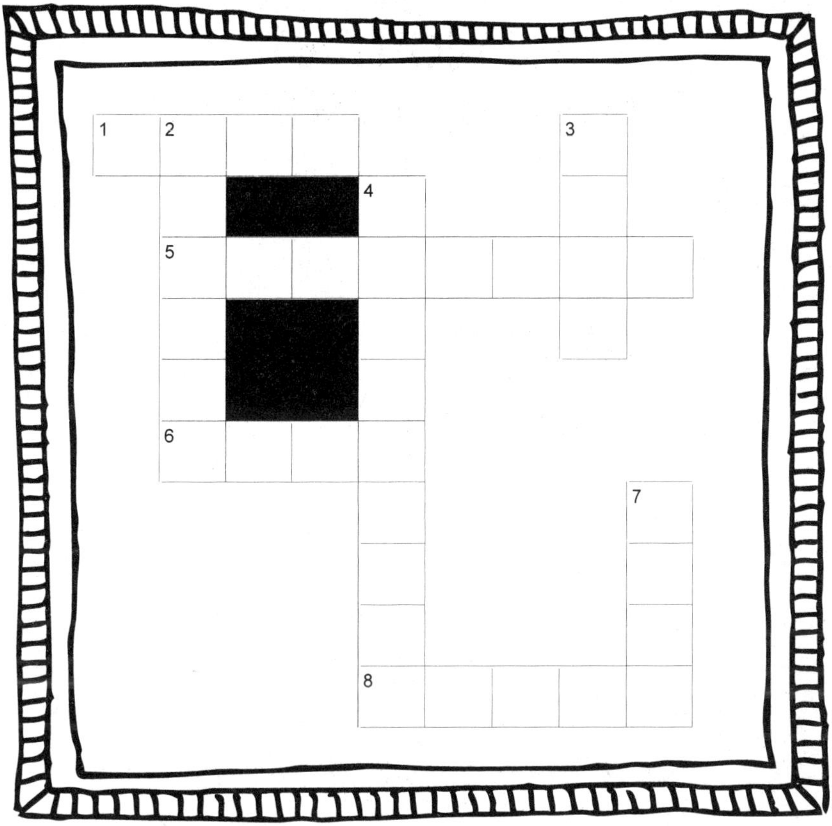

BONUS TRIVIA!

Where did baby Moses' mother hide a basket holding her little boy?

      a) in the (Nile) river
      b) in a tree top
      c) in a cave
      d) in the trunk of her car

Answer: a) in the (Nile) river (Exodus 2:3)

7. AN ALMOST-SACRIFICE
GENESIS 22:1-14

ACROSS

1. An animal was caught in this (v. 13)
4. The thing to be burnt (v. 2)
6. Abraham almost did this to his son (v. 10)
7. Animal caught by his horns (v. 13)

DOWN

1. The day Abraham saw the place afar off (v. 4)
2. One of the items Abraham carried (v. 6)
3. The name of the place where the burnt offering was to take place (v. 2)
5. The name of Abraham's son (v. 2)

8. THE STOLEN BLESSING
GENESIS 27:30-37

And it came to pass, as soon as Isaac had made an end of **blessing** Jacob, and Jacob was yet scarce gone out from the presence of Isaac his father, that **Esau** his brother came in from his hunting. And he also had made savoury meat, and brought it unto his father, and said unto his father, Let my father arise, and eat of his son's venison, that thy soul may bless me. And Isaac his father said unto him, Who art thou? And he said, I am thy son, thy **firstborn** Esau. And Isaac **trembled** very exceedingly, and said, Who? where is he that hath taken venison, and brought it me, and I have eaten of all before thou camest, and have blessed him? yea, and he shall be blessed. And when Esau heard the words of his father, he cried with a great and exceeding **bitter** cry, and said unto his father, Bless me, even me also, O my father. And he said, Thy **brother** came with subtilty, and hath **taken** away thy blessing. And he said, Is not he rightly named **Jacob**? for he hath supplanted me these two times: he **took** away my birthright; and, behold, now he hath taken away my blessing. And he said, Hast thou not **reserved** a blessing for me? And Isaac answered and said unto Esau, Behold, I have made him thy **lord**, and all his brethren have I given to him for servants; and with corn and wine have I sustained him: and what shall I do now unto thee, my **son**?

9. WRESTLE MANIA
GENESIS 32:24-32

And Jacob was **left alone**; and there **wrestled** a man with him until the breaking of the day. And when he saw that he prevailed not against him, he **touched** the hollow of his thigh; and the hollow of Jacob's thigh was out of **joint**, as he wrestled with him. And he said, Let me go, for the day breaketh. And he said, I will not let thee go, except thou **bless me**. And he said unto him, What is thy name? And he said, **Jacob**. And he said, Thy name shall be called no more Jacob, but **Israel**: for as a prince hast thou power with God and with men, and hast prevailed. And Jacob asked him, and said, Tell me, I pray thee, thy name. And he said, Wherefore is it that thou dost ask after my name? And he blessed him there. And Jacob called the name of the place **Peniel**: for I have seen God **face** to face, and my **life** is preserved. And as he passed over Penuel the **sun** rose upon him, and he halted upon his thigh. Therefore the children of Israel eat not of the sinew which shrank, which is upon the hollow of the **thigh**, unto this day: because he touched the hollow of Jacob's thigh in the sinew that shrank.

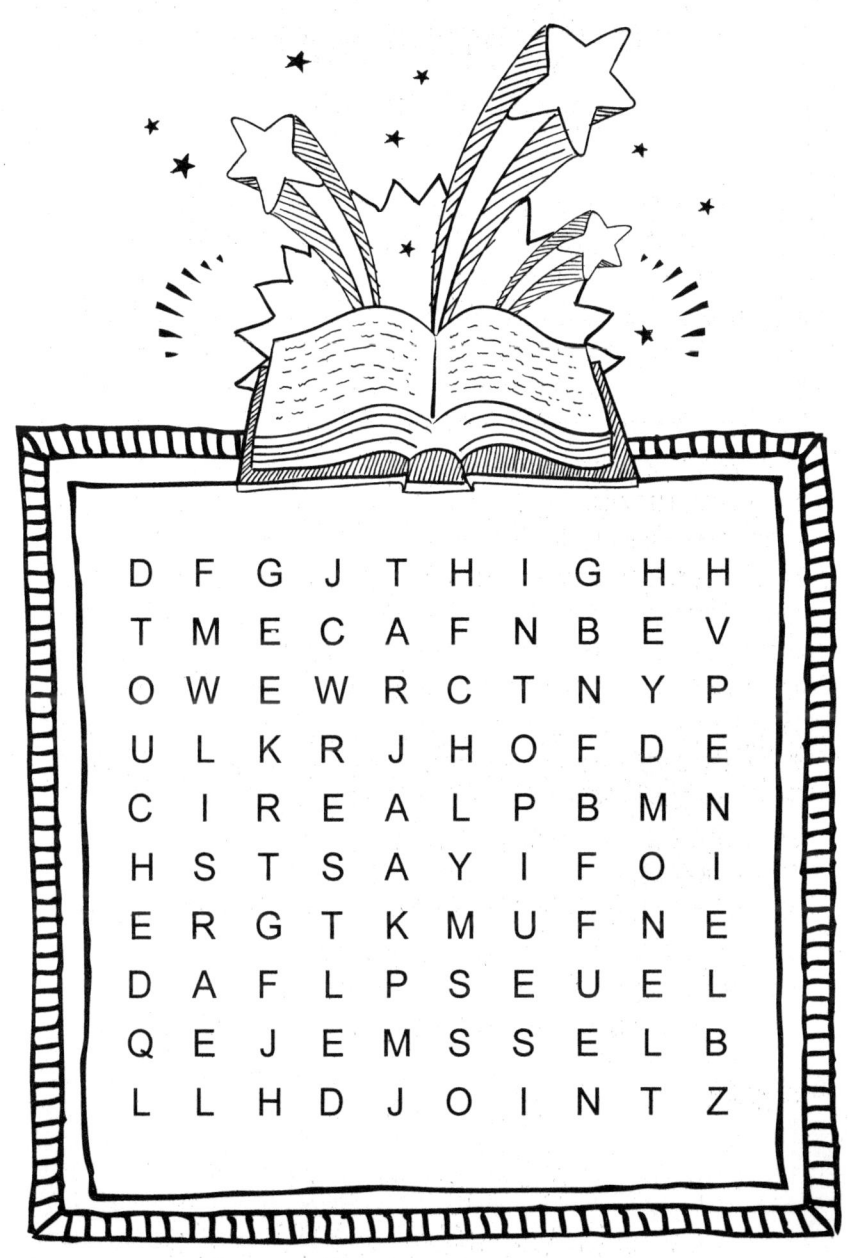

10. BETRAYED
GENESIS 37:18-28

And when they saw him afar off, even before he came near unto them, they conspired against him to slay him. And they said one to another, Behold, this **dreamer** cometh. Come now therefore, and let us slay him, and cast him into some pit, and we will say, Some evil beast hath **devoured** him: and we shall see what will become of his dreams. And Reuben heard it, and he delivered him out of their hands; and said, Let us not kill him. And Reuben said unto them, Shed no **blood**, but cast him into this pit that is in the wilderness, and lay no hand upon him; that he might rid him out of their hands, to deliver him to his father again. And it came to pass, when Joseph was come unto his brethren, that they stript Joseph out of his coat, his coat of many colours that was on him; And they took him, and cast him into a pit: and the pit was **empty**, there was no water in it. And they sat down to eat bread: and they lifted up their eyes and looked, and, behold, a company of Ishmeelites came from **Gilead** with their **camels** bearing spicery and **balm** and myrrh, going to carry it down to Egypt. And **Judah** said unto his brethren, What profit is it if we slay our brother, and conceal his blood? Come, and let us **sell** him to the Ishmeelites, and let not our hand be upon him; for he is our brother and our flesh. And his brethren were content. Then there passed by Midianites merchantmen; and they drew and lifted up Joseph out of the pit, and sold Joseph to the Ishmeelites for **twenty** pieces of **silver**: and they brought Joseph into **Egypt**.

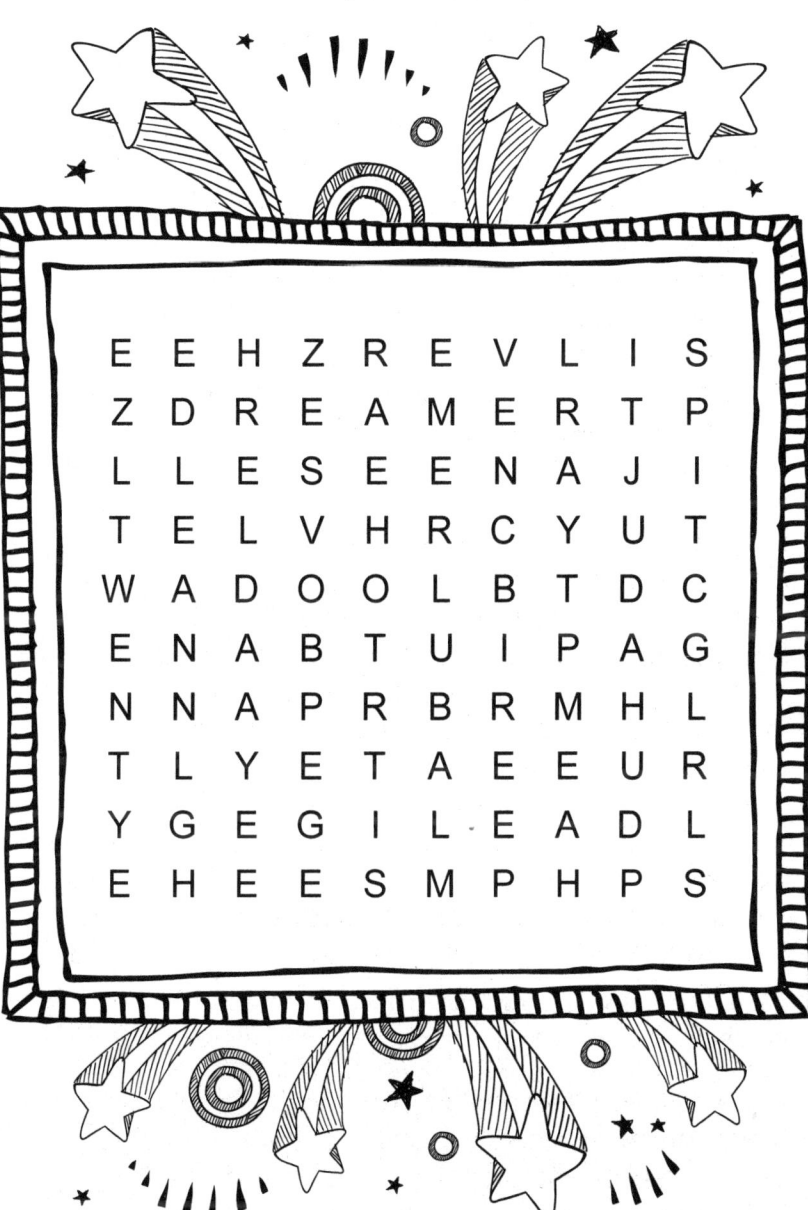

11. MOSES' CALLING
EXODUS 3:1-10

ACROSS

2. God promised a land of milk and this (v. 8)

3. Another name for the mountain of God (v. 1)

5. Moses kept and tended this (v. 1)

6. The place where Moses led sheep (v. 1)

DOWN

1. Moses' father-in-law (v. 1)

2. The type of ground Moses stood on (v. 5)

4. Moses saw this burning, but not burning up (v. 2)

5. What makes something burn (v. 2)

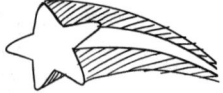 **BONUS TRIVIA!**

What made King Saul stand out from rest of the Israelites?

    a) He was stronger.
    b) He had darker skin.
    c) He was taller.
    d) He had a nicer voice.

Answer: c) He was taller. (1 Samuel 9:2)

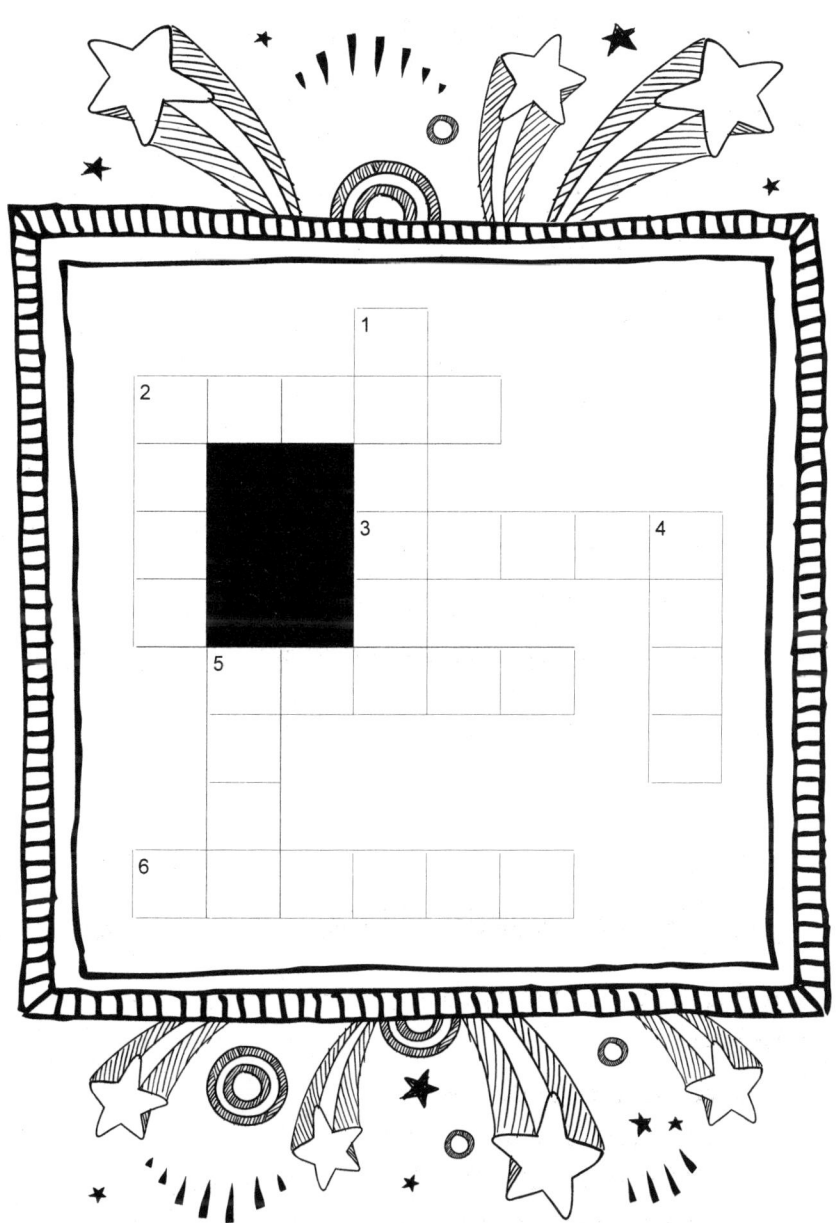

12. PASSED OVER
EXODUS 12:27-30

That ye shall say, It is the sacrifice of the Lord's **passover**, who passed over the houses of the children of Israel in Egypt, when he smote the Egyptians, and delivered our houses. And the people **bowed** the head and worshipped. And the children of Israel went away, and did as the Lord had commanded Moses and Aaron, so did they. And it came to pass, that at **midnight** the Lord smote all the **firstborn** in the land of **Egypt**, from the firstborn of Pharaoh that sat on his **throne** unto the firstborn of the captive that was in the **dungeon**; and all the firstborn of cattle. And **Pharaoh** rose up in the **night**, he, and all his servants, and all the Egyptians; and there was a great **cry** in Egypt; for there was not a **house** where there was not one **dead**.

13. PARTING OF THE RED SEA
EXODUS 14:21-31

ACROSS

1. The children of this nation saw God's miraculous power (v. 29)

3. Moses stretched this out over the waters (v. 21)

6. The people who pursued the Israelites (v. 23)

7. One of the things the water covered when it returned to its place (v. 28)

8. A direction mentioned in this story (v. 21)

9. The Lord used this to part the waters (v. 21)

DOWN

2. What God commanded Moses to stretch his hand over (v. 26)

4. What the seabed was like when the Israelites walked on it (v. 22)

5. The waters miraculously became this (v. 21)

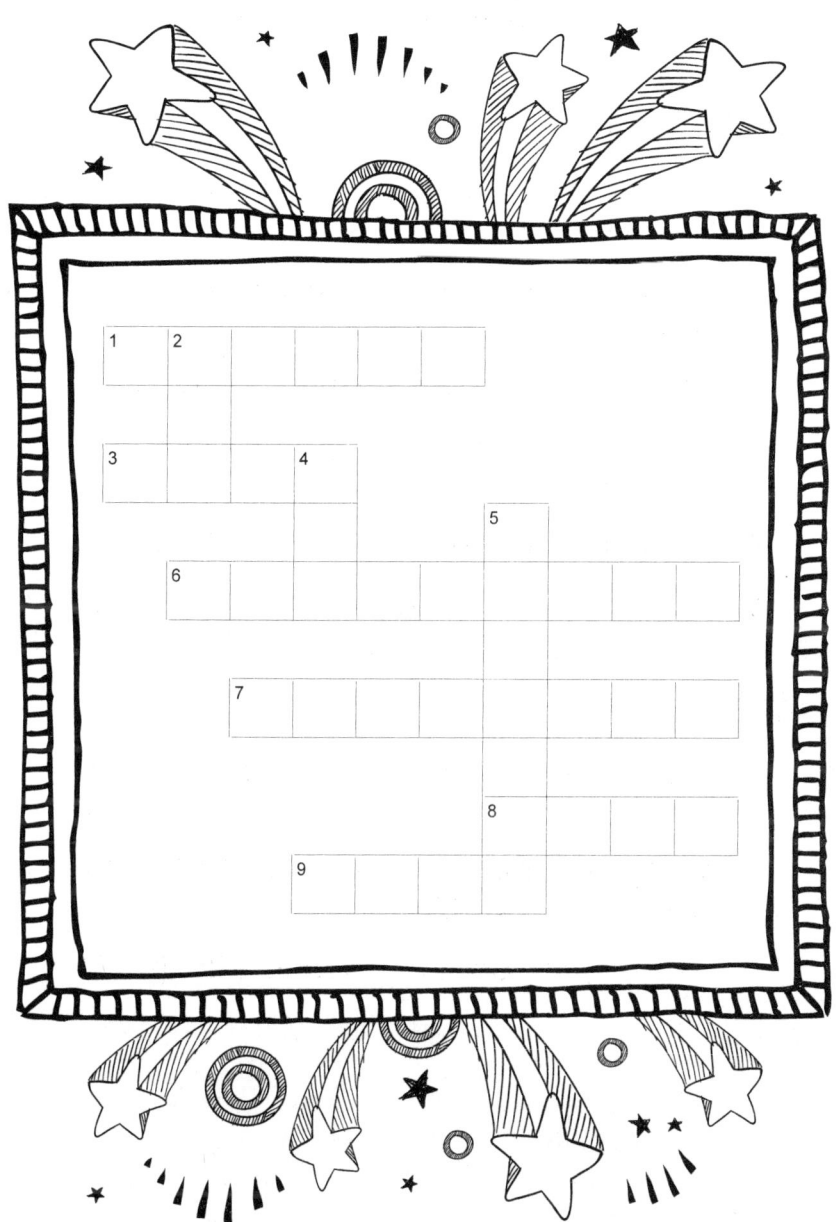

14. THE TEN COMMANDMENTS
EXODUS 20:1-17

And God **spake** all these words, saying, I am the Lord thy God, which have brought thee out of the land of Egypt, out of the house of bondage. Thou shalt have **no other** gods before me. Thou shalt not make unto thee any graven image, or any likeness of any thing that is in heaven above, or that is in the earth beneath, or that is in the water under the earth. Thou shalt **not bow** down thyself to them, nor serve them: for I the Lord thy God am a jealous God. . . . Shewing mercy unto thousands of them that love me, and keep my commandments. Thou shalt not take the **name** of the Lord thy God in vain; for the Lord will not hold him guiltless that taketh his name in vain. Remember the sabbath day, to keep it **holy**. Six days shalt thou labour, and do all thy work: But the **seventh** day is the sabbath of the Lord thy God: in it thou shalt not do any work, thou, nor thy son, nor thy daughter, thy manservant, nor thy maidservant, nor thy cattle, nor thy stranger that is within thy gates: For in **six** days the Lord made heaven and earth, the sea, and all that in them is, and **rested** the seventh day: wherefore the Lord blessed the sabbath day, and hallowed it. Honour thy father and thy **mother**: that thy days may be long upon the land which the Lord thy God giveth thee. Thou shalt not kill. Thou shalt not commit adultery. Thou shalt **not steal**. Thou shalt not bear false witness against thy neighbour. Thou shalt **not covet** thy neighbour's house, thou shalt not covet thy neighbour's wife, nor his manservant, nor his maidservant, nor his ox. . .nor any thing that is thy neighbour's.

15. THE GOLDEN CALF
EXODUS 32:1-9

And when the people saw that Moses **delayed** to come down out of the mount, the people **gathered** themselves together unto Aaron, and said unto him, Up, make us gods, which shall go before us; for as for this Moses, the man that brought us up out of the land of Egypt, we wot not what is become of him. And **Aaron** said unto them, Break off the **golden** earrings, which are in the ears of your wives, of your sons, and of your daughters, and bring them unto me. And all the people brake off the golden earrings which were in their ears, and brought them unto Aaron. And he received them at their hand, and fashioned it with a graving **tool**, after he had made it a molten **calf**: and they said, These be thy gods, O Israel, which brought thee up out of the land of Egypt. And when Aaron saw it, he **built** an **altar** before it; and Aaron made proclamation, and said, To morrow is a feast to the Lord. And they rose up early on the morrow, and offered burnt offerings, and brought peace offerings; and the people sat down to **eat** and to drink, and rose up to **play**. And the Lord said unto **Moses**, Go, get thee down; for thy people, which thou broughtest out of the land of Egypt, have corrupted themselves: They have turned aside quickly out of the way which I commanded them: they have made them a molten calf, and have worshipped it, and have sacrificed thereunto, and said, These be thy **gods**, O Israel, which have brought thee up out of the land of Egypt. And the Lord said unto Moses, I have seen this people, and, behold, it is a stiffnecked people.

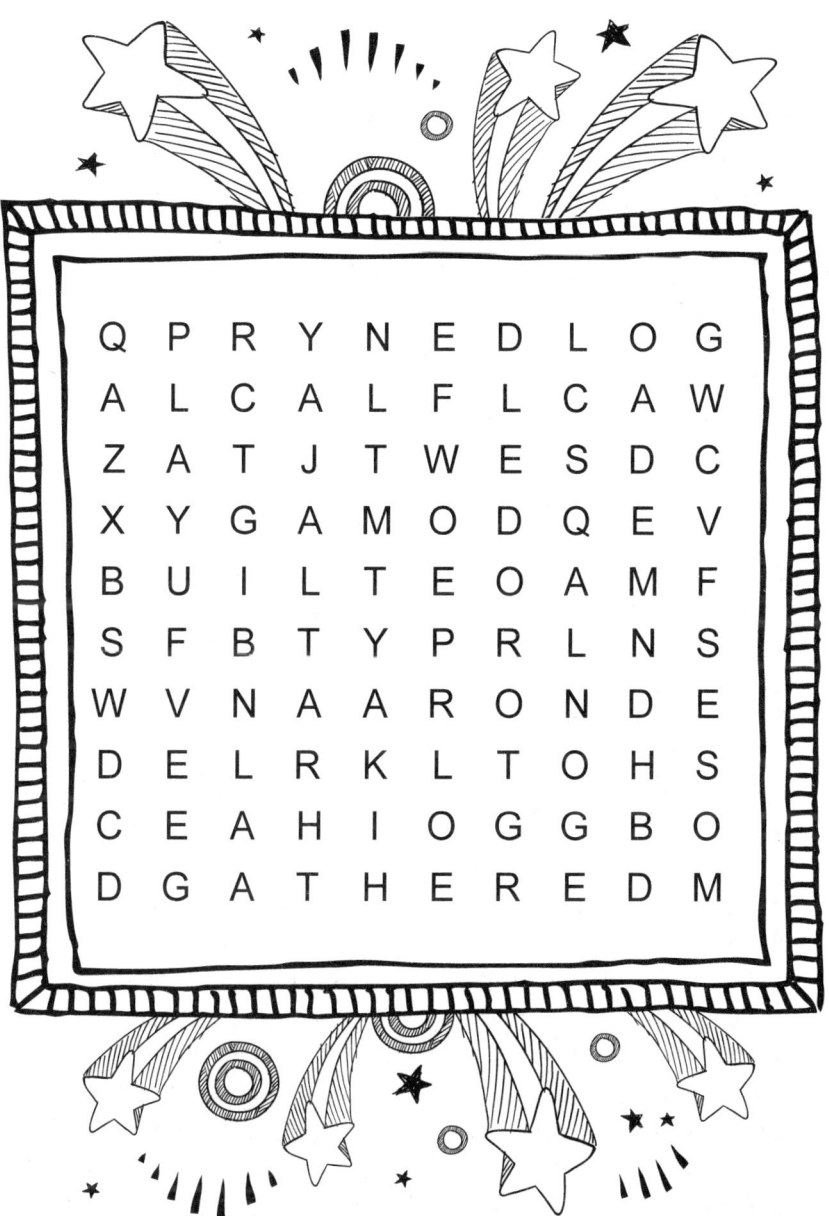

16. CONSEQUENCES OF POOR CHOICES
NUMBERS 14:20-35

ACROSS

1. What would happen to every complainer's body (v. 32)

3. The place where the people would suffer (v. 29)

6. The number of times the people tempted God (v. 22)

8. The time unit lost for each day they searched the land (v. 34)

DOWN

1. The number of years God would make the people wander (v. 34)

2. The starting age for those who would be punished (v. 29)

4. This would happen to every adult wandering in the wilderness (v. 35)

5. God would not let the people do this with the land He promised (v. 23)

7. One person God made an exception for (v. 24)

17. THE BRASS SERPENT
NUMBERS 21:4-9

And they journeyed from **mount Hor** by the way of the **Red sea**, to compass the land of **Edom**: and the soul of the people was much discouraged because of the way. And the people spake against God, and against Moses, Wherefore have ye brought us up out of Egypt to die in the wilderness? for there is no **bread**, neither is there any **water**; and our soul loatheth this light bread. And the Lord sent fiery **serpents** among the people, and they bit the people; and much people of Israel **died**. Therefore the people came to Moses, and said, We have sinned, for we have spoken against the Lord, and against thee; **pray** unto the Lord, that he take away the serpents from us. And Moses prayed for the people. And the Lord said unto Moses, Make thee a fiery serpent, and set it upon a pole: and it shall come to pass, that every one that is bitten, when he **looketh** upon it, shall **live**. And Moses made a serpent of **brass**, and put it upon a **pole**, and it came to pass, that if a serpent had bitten any man, when he beheld the serpent of brass, he lived.

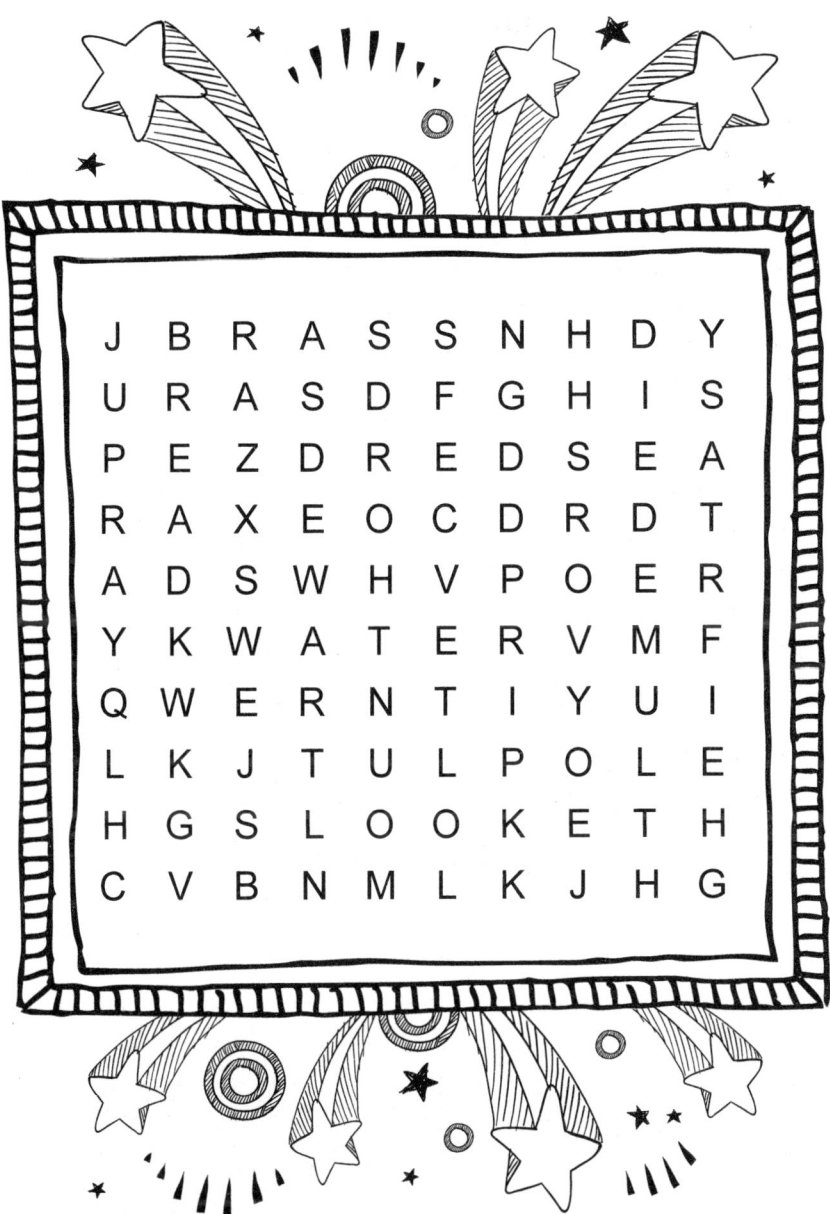

18. SUPER-STRONG CITY WALLS CRUMBLE TO DUST
JOSHUA 6:1-5

Now **Jericho** was straitly **shut** up because of the children of Israel: none went out, and none came in. And the Lord said unto **Joshua**, See, I have given into thine hand Jericho, and the king thereof, and the mighty men of valour. And ye shall compass the city, all ye men of war, and go round about the city **once**. Thus shalt thou do **six** days. And seven **priests** shall bear before the ark seven **trumpets** of rams' horns: and the **seventh** day ye shall compass the city seven times, and the priests shall blow with the trumpets. And it shall come to pass, that when they make a long blast with the ram's horn, and when ye **hear** the sound of the trumpet, all the people shall **shout** with a great shout; and the **wall** of the city shall **fall** down flat, and the people shall ascend up every man straight before him.

```
L K J H G F D X S A
Q J W E R T I E Y S
S P O I U S Y C T E
T U H S R E H N P V
E X C B H N U O O E
P S I G E U F J U N
M W R T A W A L L T
U E E R R H L M I H
R D J F B Y L N K S
T C V P R I E S T S
```

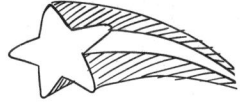 

BONUS TRIVIA!

What strange vision did Ezekiel once have?

  a) a tree in the middle of a tree
  b) a box in the middle of a box
  c) a star in the middle of a star
  d) a wheel in the middle of a wheel

Answer: d) a wheel in the middle of a wheel (Ezekiel 1:16)

19. TREATY WITH DECEIVERS
JOSHUA 9:3-27

ACROSS

1. The place where the deceivers lived (v. 3)

5. The deceivers were made to draw and carry this (v. 27)

6. Joshua made this type of treaty with the deceivers (v. 15)

7. The number of days it took Joshua to learn of the deception (v. 16)

8. The first old, worn-out items the deceivers loaded (v. 4)

DOWN

2. The item that was dry and moldy (v. 5)

3. What the Israelites could not do because of the treaty before the Lord (two words, v. 19)

4. The deceivers agreed to be this to the Israelites (v. 11)

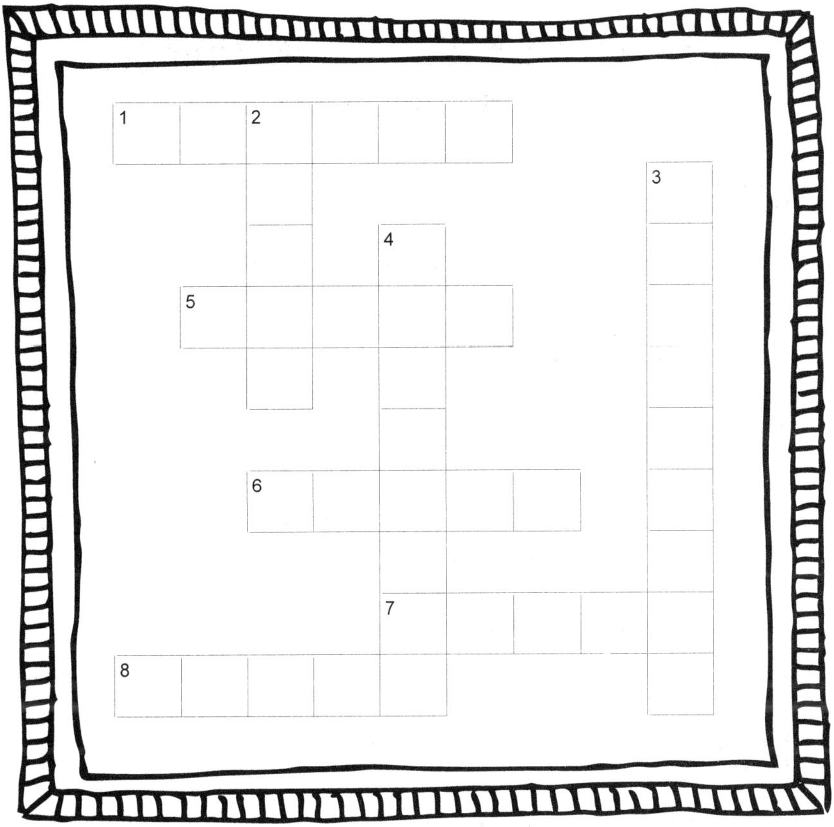

 **BONUS TRIVIA!**

What man's wife turned into a pillar of salt after disobeying God?

    a) Lot
    b) Moses
    c) Peter
    d) Ronald McDonald

Answer: a) Lot (Genesis 19:18–26)

20. THE DAY THE SUN DID NOT MOVE
JOSHUA 10:7-15

So Joshua ascended from **Gilgal**, he, and all the people of war with him, and all the mighty men of valour. And the Lord said unto Joshua, Fear them not: for I have delivered them into thine hand; there shall not a man of them stand before thee. Joshua therefore came unto them suddenly, and went up from Gilgal all **night**. And the Lord discomfited them before Israel, and slew them with a great slaughter at Gibeon, and **chased** them along the way that goeth up to Bethhoron, and smote them to Azekah, and unto Makkedah. And it came to pass, as they **fled** from before Israel, and were in the going down to Bethhoron, that the Lord cast down great stones from heaven upon them unto Azekah, and they died: they were more which died with **hailstones** than they whom the children of Israel slew with the sword. Then spake **Joshua** to the Lord in the day when the Lord delivered up the Amorites before the children of Israel, and he said in the sight of Israel, **Sun**, stand thou still upon Gibeon; and thou, **Moon**, in the valley of Ajalon. And the sun stood still, and the moon stayed, until the people had avenged themselves upon their enemies. Is not this written in the book of **Jasher**? So the sun <u>stood still</u> in the midst of heaven, and hasted not to go down about a whole day. And there was no day like that before it or after it, that the Lord hearkened unto the **voice** of a man: for the Lord fought for Israel. And Joshua returned, and all Israel with him, unto the camp to Gilgal.

21. 300 MEN (AND THE LORD) VS. A HUGE ARMY
JUDGES 7:15–22

And it was so, when **Gideon** heard the telling of the **dream**, and the interpretation thereof, that he worshipped, and returned into the host of Israel, and said, **Arise**; for the Lord hath delivered into your hand the host of **Midian**. And he divided the three hundred men into **three** companies, and he put a trumpet in every man's hand, with **empty** pitchers, and lamps within the pitchers. And he said unto them, Look on me, and do likewise: and, behold, when I come to the outside of the camp, it shall be that, as I do, so shall ye do. When I blow with a **trumpet**, I and all that are with me, then blow ye the trumpets also on every side of all the camp, and say, The sword of the Lord, and of Gideon. So Gideon, and the **hundred** men that were with him, came unto the outside of the **camp** in the beginning of the middle watch; and they had but newly set the watch: and they blew the trumpets, and brake the pitchers that were in their hands. And the three companies blew the trumpets, and brake the pitchers, and held the lamps in their left hands, and the trumpets in their right hands to blow withal: and they cried, The **sword** of the Lord, and of Gideon. And they **stood** every man in his place round about the camp; and all the host ran, and cried, and fled. And the three hundred blew the trumpets, and the Lord set every man's sword against his fellow, even throughout all the host: and the host **fled** to Bethshittah in Zererath, and to the border of Abelmeholah, unto Tabbath.

22. A HAIRY SITUATION
JUDGES 16:13-21

And **Delilah** said unto Samson, Hitherto thou hast **mocked** me, and told me **lies**: tell me wherewith thou mightest be bound. And he said unto her, If thou weavest the seven locks of my head with the web. And she fastened it with the pin, and said unto him, The Philistines be upon thee, **Samson**. And he awaked out of his sleep, and went away with the pin of the beam, and with the web. And she said unto him, How canst thou say, I love thee, when thine heart is not with me? thou hast mocked me these three times, and hast not told me wherein thy great **strength** lieth. And it came to pass, when she pressed him daily. . .that he told her all his heart, and said unto her, There hath not come a **razor** upon mine head; for I have been a **Nazarite** unto God from my mother's womb: if I be shaven, then my strength will go from me, and I shall become weak, and be like any other man. And when Delilah saw that he had told her all his heart, she sent and called for the lords of the Philistines. . . . Then the lords of the Philistines came up unto her, and brought money in their hand. And she made him sleep upon her knees; and she called for a man, and she caused him to **shave** off the **seven** locks of his head; and she began to afflict him, and his strength went from him. And she said, The Philistines be upon thee, Samson. And he awoke out of his sleep, and said, I will go out as at other times before, and shake myself. And he wist not that the Lord was departed from him. But the Philistines took him, and put out his **eyes**, and brought him down to **Gaza**, and bound him with fetters of brass; and he did grind in the **prison** house.

23. IDOL MYSTERIOUSLY BOWS BEFORE THE LORD'S ARK
1 SAMUEL 5:1-5

And the Philistines took the ark of God, and brought it from **Ebenezer** unto **Ashdod**. When the Philistines took the **ark** of God, they brought it into the house of Dagon, and set it by Dagon. And when they of Ashdod arose early on the morrow, behold, Dagon was fallen upon his face to the earth before the ark of the Lord. And they took Dagon, and set him in his place again. And when they arose early on the morrow **morning**, behold, Dagon was **fallen** upon his **face** to the **ground** before the ark of the Lord; and the **head** of Dagon and both the **palms** of his **hands** were cut off upon the threshold; only the stump of Dagon was left to him. Therefore neither the priests of **Dagon**, nor any that come into Dagon's house, tread on the **threshold** of Dagon in Ashdod unto this day.

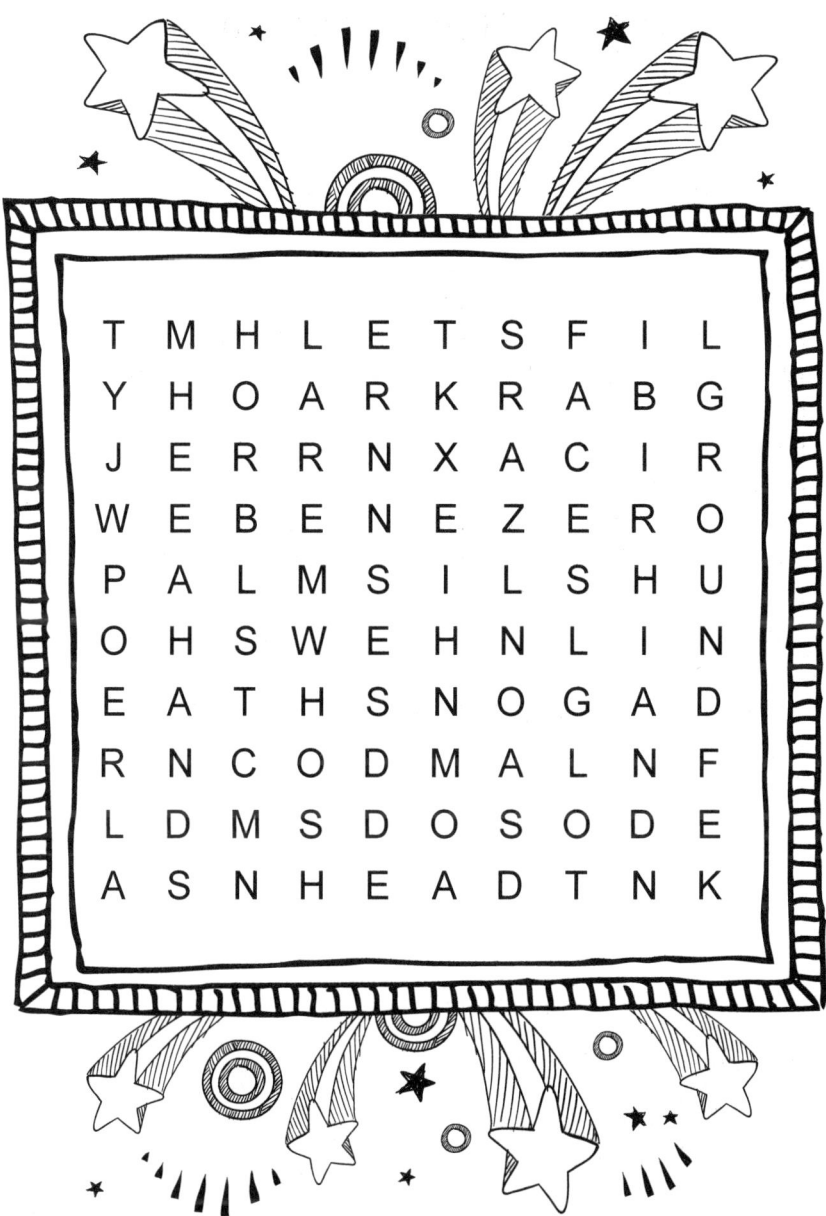

24. GOLIATH!
1 SAMUEL 17:4-7

And there went out a **champion** out of the camp of the Philistines, named **Goliath**, of Gath, whose height was six cubits and a span. And he had an **helmet** of **brass** upon his head, and he was **armed** with a **coat of mail**; and the weight of the coat was five thousand shekels of brass. And he had **greaves** of brass upon his **legs**, and a target of brass between his **shoulders**. And the staff of his **spear** was like a weaver's beam; and his spear's head weighed six hundred shekels of **iron**: and one bearing a **shield** went before him.

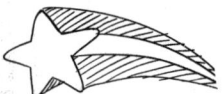 **BONUS TRIVIA!**

What kind of animal spoke to a prophet named Balaam?

    a) a platypus
    b) a dog
    c) a lion
    d) a donkey

Answer: d) a donkey (Numbers 22:28)

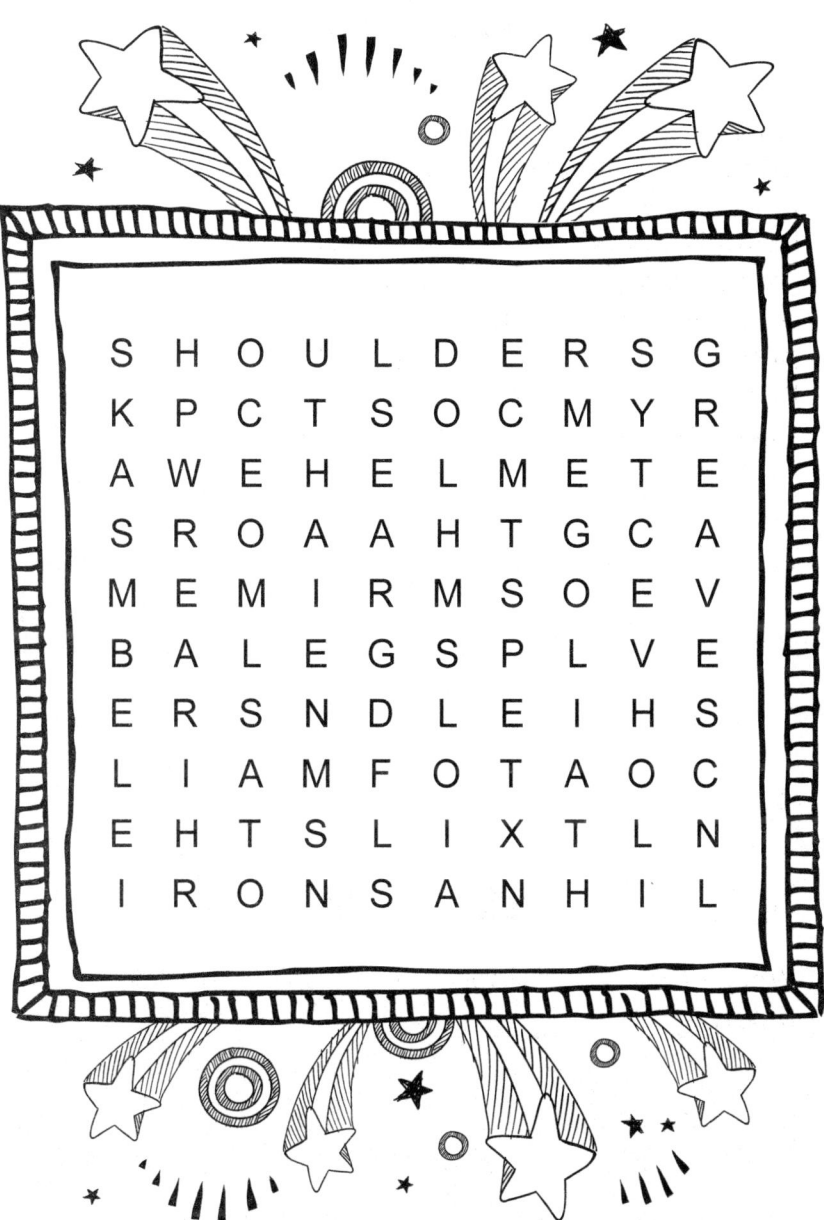

25. DAVID AND GOLIATH
1 SAMUEL 17:8-26

ACROSS

1. Goliath's nationality (v. 10)
4. David's father (v. 12)
6. What David's brothers were ready to fight (v. 13)
8. How Israel's soldiers felt about Goliath (v. 11)

DOWN

2. David's country (v. 10)
3. Animals David watched (v. 15)
5. King of Israel (v. 8)
7. Fighting group of Israel or its enemy (v. 21)

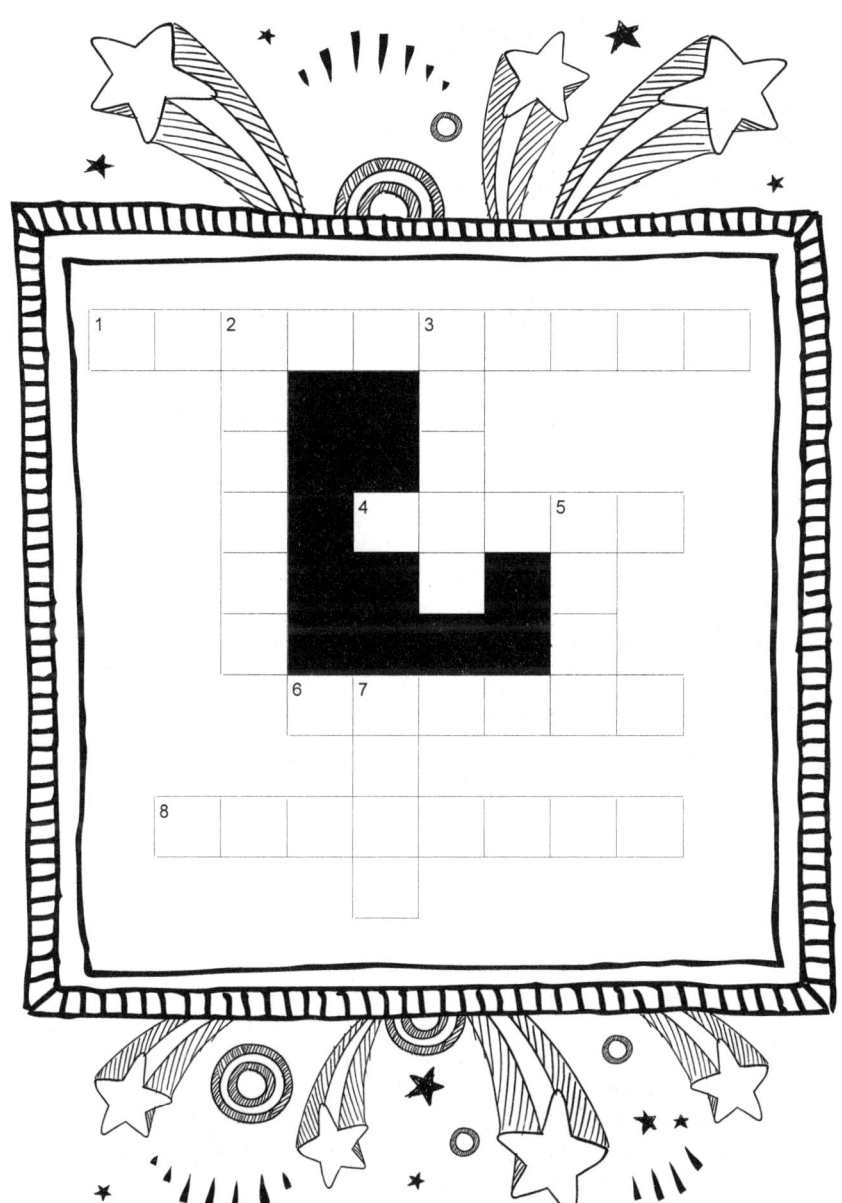

26. DAVID AND SAUL
1 SAMUEL 24:1-18

ACROSS

2. What Saul was to the Lord (v. 6)

5. What David did to Saul's life (v. 10)

8. Animals that lived on the rocks and crags (two words, v. 2)

DOWN

1. David had part of Saul's robe here (v. 11)

3. How many thousand men Saul had seeking David (v. 2)

4. Who was more righteous than Saul? (v. 17)

6. What David did when he talked with Saul (v. 8)

7. The place where this Bible passage takes place (v. 3)

27. KING SAUL'S CREEPY NIGHT
1 SAMUEL 28:4-25

ACROSS

2. What Saul did when he saw the spirit (v. 14)

4. City that the witch lived in (v. 7)

7. The person Saul asked to bring up (v. 11)

DOWN

1. The general age of the man Saul saw (v. 14)

3. What the spirit had for Saul (v. 20)

5. The time Saul went to the woman (v. 8)

6. The animal the witch killed to serve as food (v. 24)

8. One way the Lord did not answer Saul (v. 6)

 **BONUS TRIVIA!**

What did God give Daniel the ability to explain?

    a) other languages
    b) smoke signals
    c) dreams
    d) the words in rap songs

Answer: c) dreams (Daniel 2:1–19)

28. ABSALOM
2 SAMUEL 18:9–15

And Absalom met the servants of David. And Absalom rode upon a **mule**, and the mule went under the thick boughs of a great **oak**, and his **head** caught hold of the oak, and he was taken up **between** the heaven and the earth; and the mule that was under him went away. And a certain man saw it, and told **Joab**, and said, Behold, I saw Absalom **hanged** in an oak. And Joab said unto the man that told him, And, behold, thou sawest him, and why didst thou not smite him there to the ground? and I would have given thee **ten** shekels of silver, and a girdle. And the man said unto Joab, Though I should receive a **thousand** shekels of silver in mine hand, yet would I not put forth mine hand against the king's son: for in our hearing the king charged thee and Abishai and Ittai, saying, Beware that none touch the young man **Absalom**. Otherwise I should have wrought falsehood against mine own life: for there is no matter hid from the king, and thou thyself wouldest have set thyself against me. Then said Joab, I may not tarry thus with thee. And he took **three** darts in his hand, and thrust them through the **heart** of Absalom, while he was yet **alive** in the midst of the oak. And ten young men that bare Joab's armour compassed about and smote Absalom, and slew him.

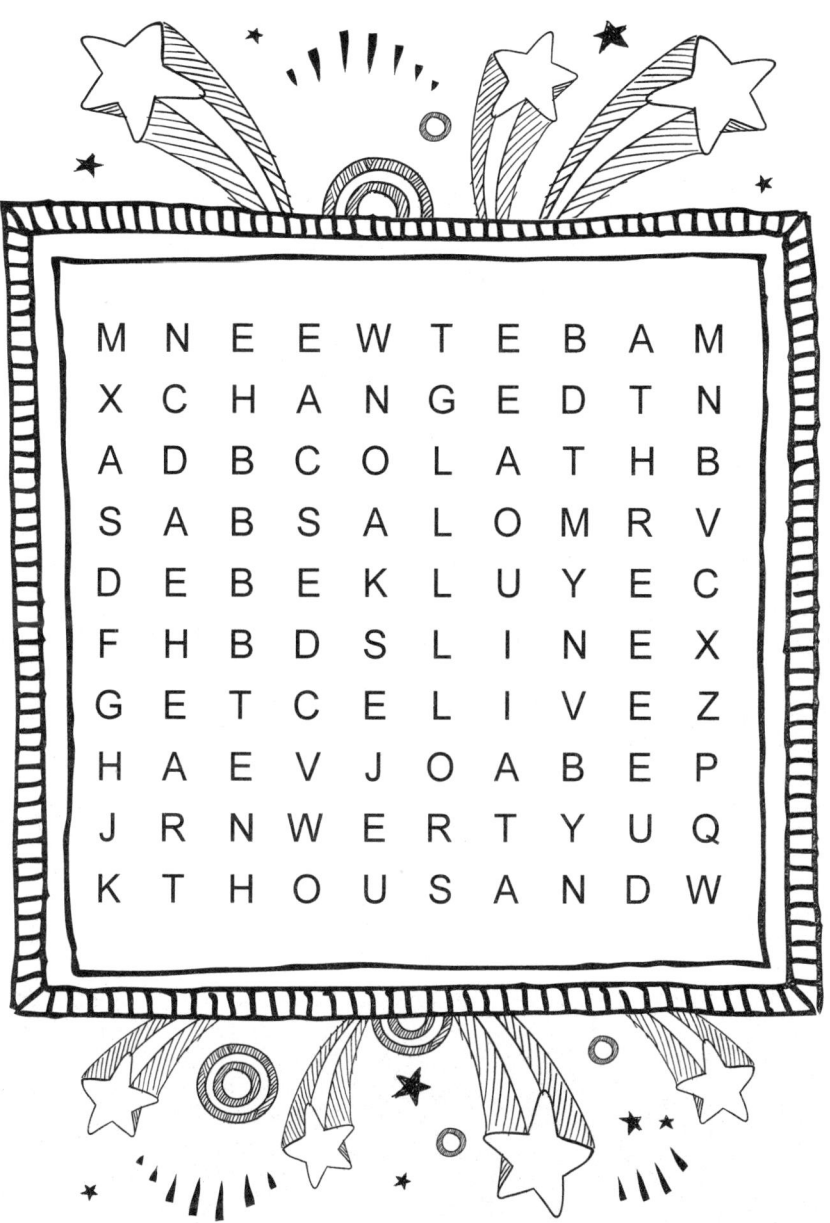

29. A YOUNG KING ASKS FOR WISDOM
1 KINGS 3:5-15

ACROSS

3. How the Lord appeared to the young king (v. 5)

5. The king was to do this in the Lord's ways (v. 14)

6. What the king gave for all of his servants (v. 15)

7. The young king's name (v. 15)

DOWN

1. This object would hold the king's wisdom (v. 12)

2. Where the Lord appeared to the king (v. 5)

4. First thing the Lord said to the king (v. 5)

5. What the king would be, along with understanding (v. 12)

30. DAILY FED BY BIRDS
1 KINGS 17:1-6

And **Elijah** the Tishbite, who was of the inhabitants of **Gilead**, said unto Ahab, As the Lord God of Israel liveth, before whom I stand, there shall not be dew nor **rain** these years, but according to my word. And the word of the Lord came unto him, saying, Get thee hence, and turn thee **eastward**, and **hide** thyself by the **brook** Cherith, that is before Jordan. And it shall be, that thou shalt drink of the brook; and I have commanded the **ravens** to **feed** thee there. So he went and did according unto the word of the Lord: for he went and dwelt by the brook Cherith, that is before Jordan. And the ravens brought him **bread** and flesh in the **morning**, and bread and **flesh** in the **evening**; and he drank of the brook.

31. True God vs. False God
1 Kings 18:20-40

ACROSS

3. Mountain where the contest happened (v. 20)

4. God's prophet took twelve of these (v. 31)

8. What God's fire did to water (two words, v. 38)

DOWN

1. What the barrels contained (v. 33)

2. Who mocked the false prophets? (v. 27)

5. What the water filled (v. 35)

6. The false god in the story (v. 26)

7. How many hundred false prophets (plus fifty more) were there? (v. 22)

32. CHARIOT OF FIRE
2 KINGS 2:11–12

And it came to pass, as they still went on, and **talked**, that, behold, there appeared a **chariot** of **fire**, and **horses** of fire, and parted them both asunder; and **Elijah** went up by a **whirlwind** into **heaven**. And **Elisha** saw it, and he cried, My father, my father, the chariot of **Israel**, and the **horsemen** thereof. And he saw him no more: and he took hold of his own **clothes**, and rent them in **two** pieces.

 **BONUS TRIVIA!**

Which of these four problems was *not* a plague on Egypt?

    a) chicken pox
    b) frogs
    c) hail
    d) locusts

Answer: a) chicken pox (Exodus 8–10)

33. THE FLOATING AXE
2 KINGS 6:1-7

And the sons of the **prophets** said unto Elisha, Behold now, the place where we dwell with thee is too strait for us. Let us go, we pray thee, unto **Jordan**, and take thence every man a beam, and let us make us a place there, where we may dwell. And he answered, **Go ye**. And one said, Be content, I pray thee, and go with thy servants. And he answered, I will go. So he went with them. And when they came to Jordan, they cut down **wood**. But as one was felling a beam, the **axe head** fell into the **water**: and he cried, and said, Alas, master! for it was **borrowed**. And the man of God said, Where fell it? And he shewed him the place. And he cut down a **stick**, and cast it in thither; and the **iron** did **swim**. Therefore said he, Take it up to thee. And he put out his **hand**, and **took** it.

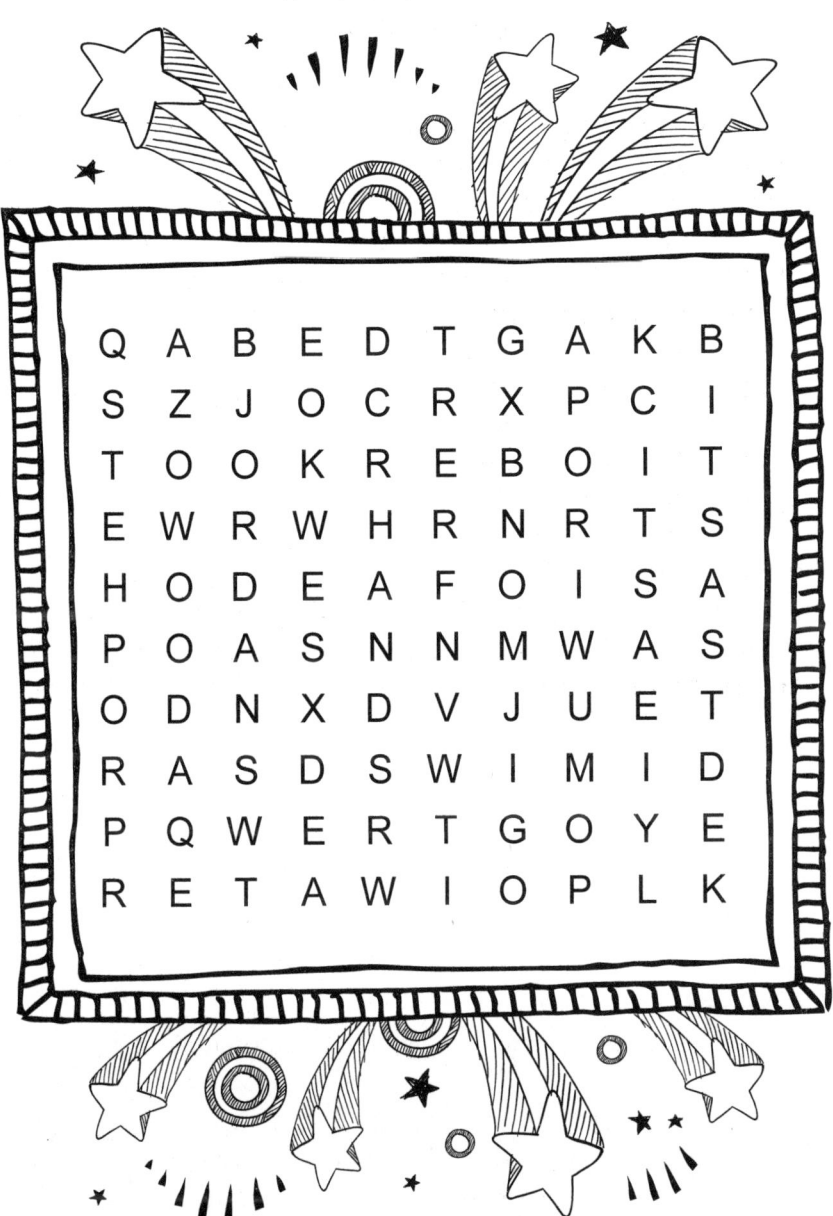

34. A KING SHOWS OFF FOR FOREIGNERS
2 KINGS 20:12–19

At that time Berodachbaladan, the son of Baladan, king of Babylon, sent **letters** and a present unto Hezekiah: for he had **heard** that Hezekiah had been **sick**. And Hezekiah hearkened unto them, and shewed them all the house of his precious things, the **silver**, and the **gold**, and the **spices**, and the precious ointment, and all the house of his armour, and all that was found in his treasures: there was **nothing** in his house, nor in all his dominion, that Hezekiah shewed them not. Then came **Isaiah** the **prophet** unto **king** Hezekiah, and said unto him, What said these men? and from whence came they unto thee? And Hezekiah said, They are come from a far country, even from Babylon. And he said, What have they seen in thine house? And Hezekiah answered, All the things that are in mine house have they seen: there is nothing among my treasures that I have not shewed them. And Isaiah said unto Hezekiah, Hear the word of the Lord. Behold, the days come, that all that is in thine house, and that which thy fathers have laid up in store unto this day, shall be carried into **Babylon**: nothing shall be left, saith the Lord. And of thy sons that shall issue from thee, which thou shalt beget, shall they take away; and they shall be eunuchs in the palace of the king of Babylon. Then said **Hezekiah** unto Isaiah, Good is the word of the Lord which thou hast spoken. And he said, Is it not good, if peace and truth be in my days?

35. NO EARTHLY PROTECTION
EZRA 8:21–23

Then I **proclaimed** a **fast** there, at the river of **Ahava**, that we might **afflict** ourselves before our God, to seek of him a **right** way for us, and for our **little ones**, and for all our substance. For I was **ashamed** to require of the **king** a band of soldiers and **horsemen** to help us against the **enemy** in the way: because we had spoken unto the king, saying, The **hand** of our God is upon all them for **good** that seek him; but his **power** and his wrath is against all them that forsake him. So we fasted and besought our God for this: and he was **intreated** of us.

```
A F F L I C T A F A
G H J T N G S E A H
Y O T O T N B U S A
M R O H R I G H T V
L S Y D E K S A H A
D E M I A L C O R P
I M E E T P O W E R
S E N O E L T T I L
C N E L D H E N M K
A S H A M E D N A H
```

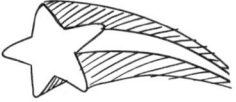 **BONUS TRIVIA!**

What had happened to the man who was helped by the Good Samaritan?

    a) He had been struck by lightning.
    b) He had fallen over a cliff.
    c) He had been bitten by a snake.
    d) He had been beaten by robbers.

Answer: d) He had been beaten by robbers. (Luke 10:30)

36. NEHEMIAH AND THE BULLIES
NEHEMIAH 6:10-14

Afterward I came unto the **house** of Shemaiah the son of Delaiah the son of Mehetabeel, who was <u>**shut up**</u>; and he said, Let us meet together in the <u>**house of God**</u>, within the temple, and let us shut the doors of the **temple**: for they will come to slay thee; yea, in the night will they come to slay thee. And I said, Should such a man as I **flee**? and who is there, that, being as I am, would go into the temple to save his life? I will not go in. And, lo, I **perceived** that God had not sent him; but that he pronounced this **prophecy** against me: for Tobiah and Sanballat had hired him. Therefore was he **hired**, that I should be **afraid**, and do so, and sin, and that they might have matter for an <u>**evil report**</u>, that they might reproach me. My God, think thou upon Tobiah and Sanballat according to these their **works**, and on the prophetess Noadiah, and the rest of the prophets, that would have put me in **fear**.

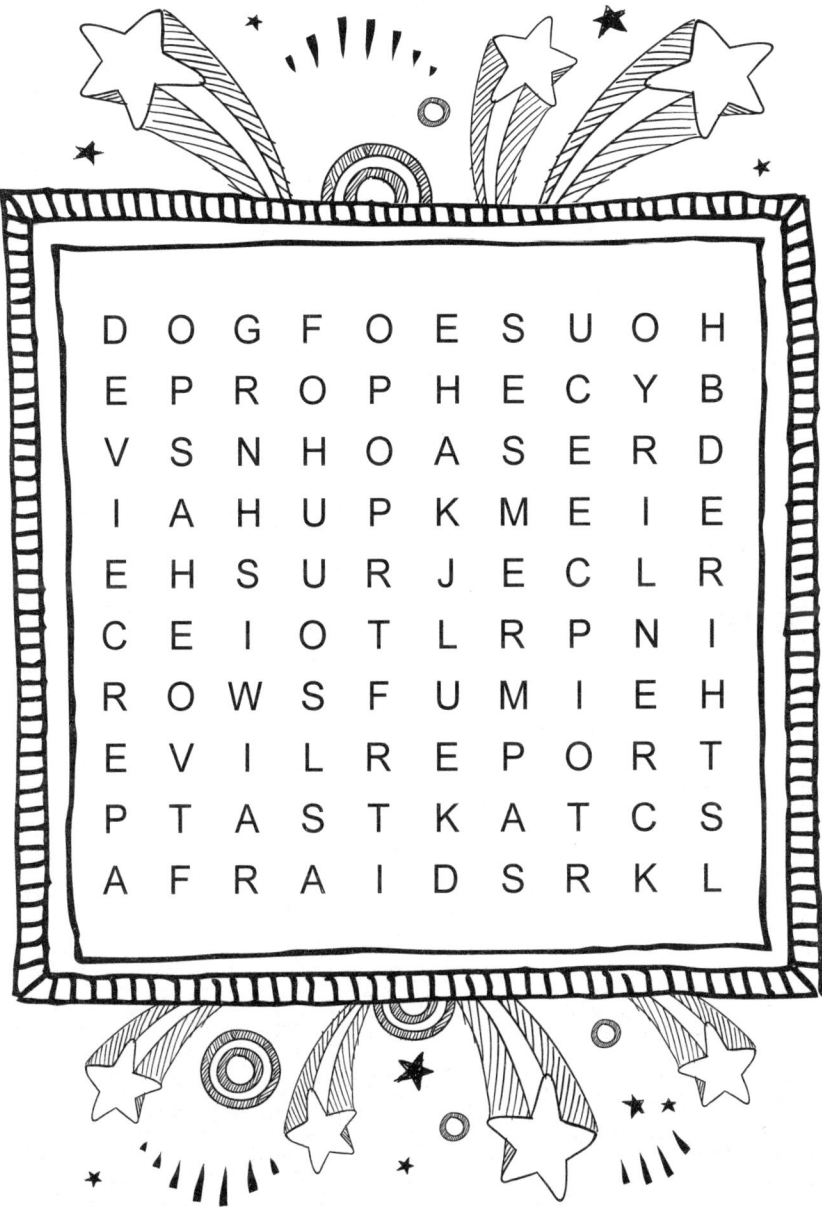

37. I'M A SHEEP!
PSALM 23:1-6

ACROSS

1. The Lord is this type of person (v. 1)
3. Sometimes we walk through this (v. 4)
5. Another name for God (v. 1)
7. What God makes us do in green pastures (v. 2)
8. It's poured out to "anoint" us (v. 5)
9. Where God leads us in righteousness (v. 3)

DOWN

1. The hint of death (v. 4)
2. The part of the body that's anointed (v. 5)
4. God prepares a table in whose presence? (v. 5)
6. Time measure of goodness and mercy (v. 6)

38. A TEST WITHOUT ROYAL FOOD
DANIEL 1:1-16

ACROSS

1. What Melzar the guard did with the meat and wine (two words, v. 16)
6. The number of years the king ordered the Israelites to eat his food (v. 5)
7. The place where the Israelites were to stand and serve the king (v. 4)
8. What the prince of the eunuchs was afraid of losing (two words, v. 10)
9. The number of days the Israelites' test was to last (v. 12)

DOWN

2. Liquid to drink during the test (v. 12)
3. What the Israelites did not want the king's food to do to them (v. 8)
4. How often the king wanted the Israelites to eat his food (v. 5)
5. The original Hebrew name for Belteshazzar (v. 7)

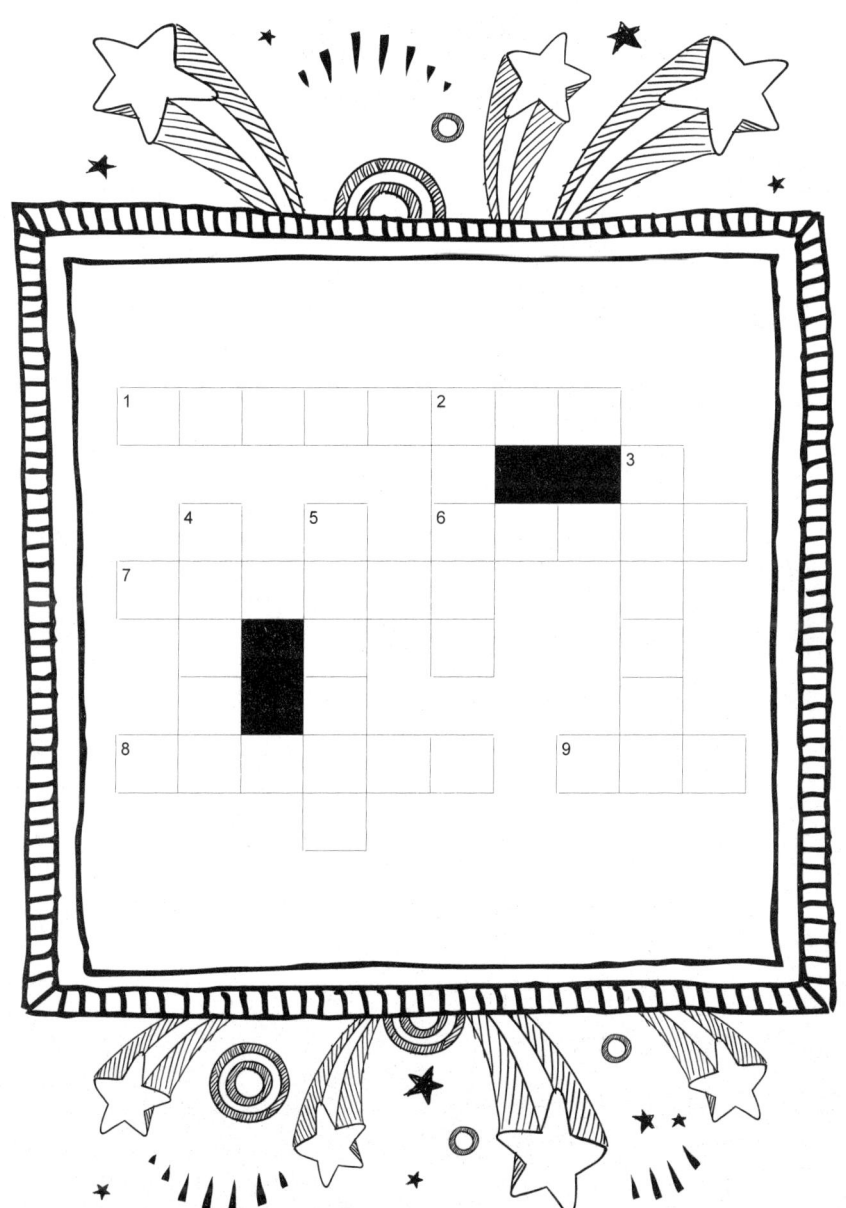

39. MYSTERIOUS WRITING ON A WALL
DANIEL 5:1-30

ACROSS

2. Third word on the wall (v. 28)

3. What God did on the wall (v. 5)

5. What part of the king knocked against each other? (v. 6)

7. Object that appeared out of nowhere (v. 5)

DOWN

1. First word on the wall (v. 26)

3. Place where the writing was found (v. 5)

4. Second word on the wall (v. 27)

6. "In that night was Belshazzar the king of the Chaldeans ____" (v. 30)

40. THE BIG CATS
DANIEL 6:4-28

ACROSS

2. How many days the people were to pray to the king (v. 7)

5. What was signed and published? (v. 12)

6. Name of the good man put in a dangerous place (v. 16)

9. Object used to cover the dangerous place (v. 17)

DOWN

1. What the good man did, to God (v. 10)

3. Number of times a day the good man honored God (v. 10)

4. What held the big cats? (v. 7)

5. Name of the king (v. 9)

7. Who shut the big cats' mouths? (v. 22)

8. What kind of big cats were they? (v. 16)

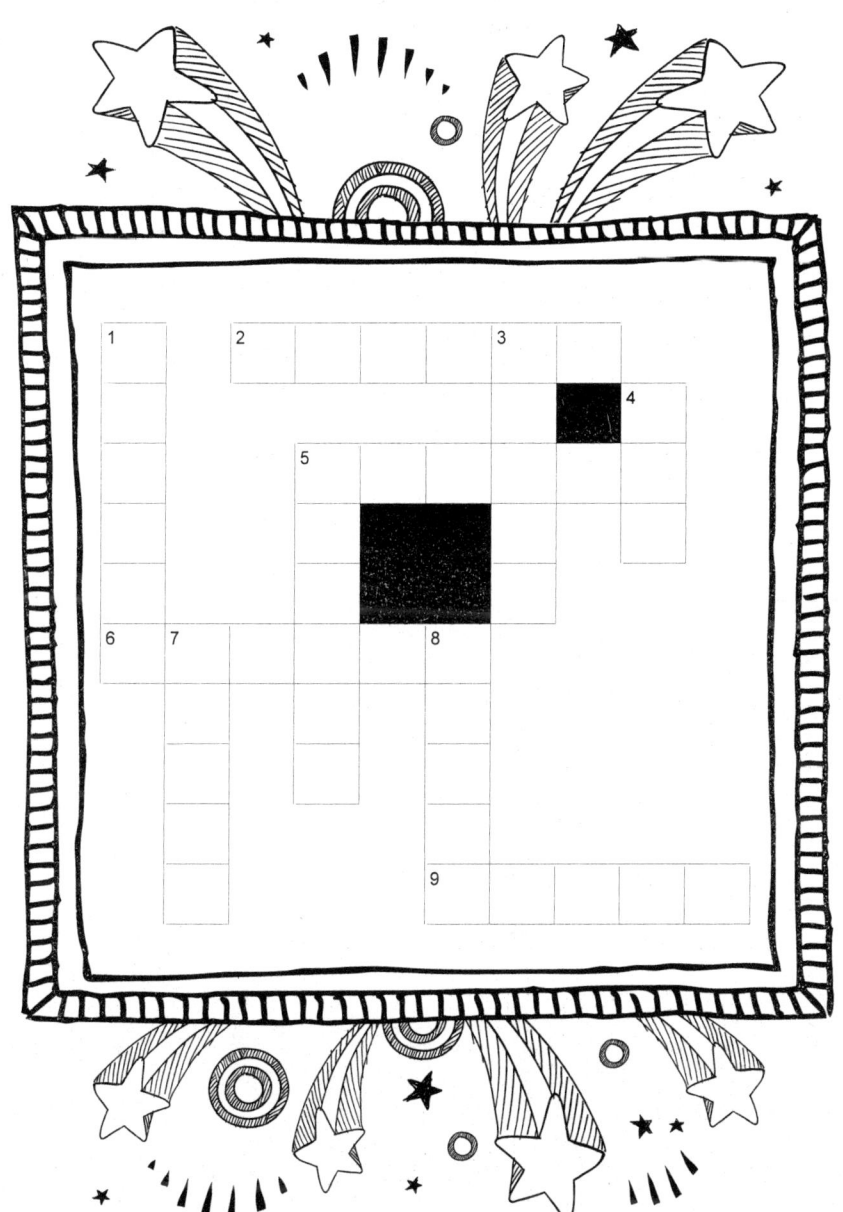

41. BIG FISH SWALLOWS LITTLE GUY
JONAH 1:1–17

ACROSS

2. What was going to Tarshish? (v. 3)

4. The word of the Lord came to this prophet (v. 1)

7. All the mariners and sailors were this (v. 5)

8. The prophet's nationality (v. 9)

DOWN

1. Creature the Lord prepared to catch the prophet (v. 17)

3. The Lord sent this out onto the sea (v. 4)

5. The place the Lord commanded the prophet to go (v. 2)

6. What the creature did to the prophet (v. 17)

42. A MUTE LESSON
LUKE 1:11-22

And there appeared unto him an **angel** of the Lord standing on the **right** side of the altar of incense. And when Zacharias saw him, he was troubled, and fear fell upon him. But the angel said unto him, Fear not, Zacharias: for thy prayer is heard; and thy wife **Elisabeth** shall bear thee a **son**, and thou shalt call his name John. And thou shalt have joy and gladness; and many shall rejoice at his birth. For he shall be **great** in the sight of the Lord, and shall drink neither wine nor strong drink; and he shall be filled with the Holy Ghost, even from his mother's womb. And many of the children of Israel shall he turn to the Lord their God. And he shall go before him in the spirit and power of Elias, to turn the hearts of the fathers to the children, and the disobedient to the wisdom of the just; to make ready a people prepared for the Lord. And Zacharias said unto the angel, Whereby shall I know this? for I am an **old** man, and my **wife** well stricken in years. And the angel answering said unto him, I am **Gabriel**, that **stand** in the presence of God; and am sent to speak unto thee, and to shew thee these glad tidings. And, behold, thou shalt be dumb, and not able to **speak**, until the day that these things shall be performed, because thou believest not my words, which shall be fulfilled in their season. And the people waited for Zacharias, and marvelled that he tarried so long in the **temple**. And when he came out, he could not speak unto them: and they perceived that he had seen a **vision** in the temple: for he beckoned unto them, and remained speechless.

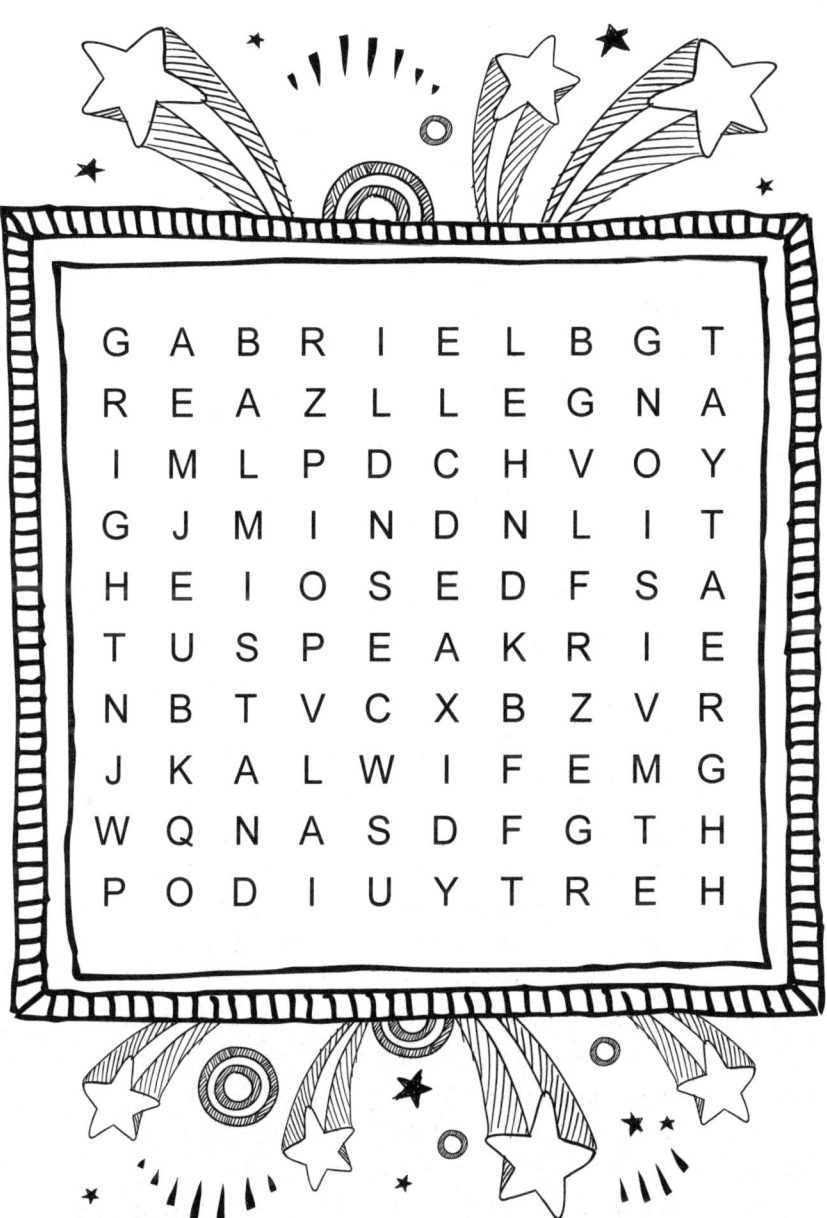

43. BABY JESUS' FIRST VISITORS
LUKE 2:8-14

ACROSS

2. What the glory of the Lord did around these people (v. 9)

3. First thing announced for those on earth (v. 14)

6. How Christ the Lord came to earth (v. 11)

7. What came with the good tidings? (two words, v. 10)

DOWN

1. Who appeared to baby Jesus' first visitors? (v. 9)

2. What was the visitors' job? (v. 8)

4. Word of praise spoken to God (v. 14)

5. What was baby Jesus lying in? (v. 12)

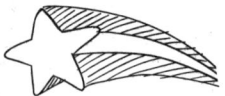 **BONUS TRIVIA!**

What instrument did David play to make King Saul feel better?

    a) an electric guitar
    b) a harp
    c) a trumpet
    d) a flute

Answer: b) a harp (1 Samuel 16:23)

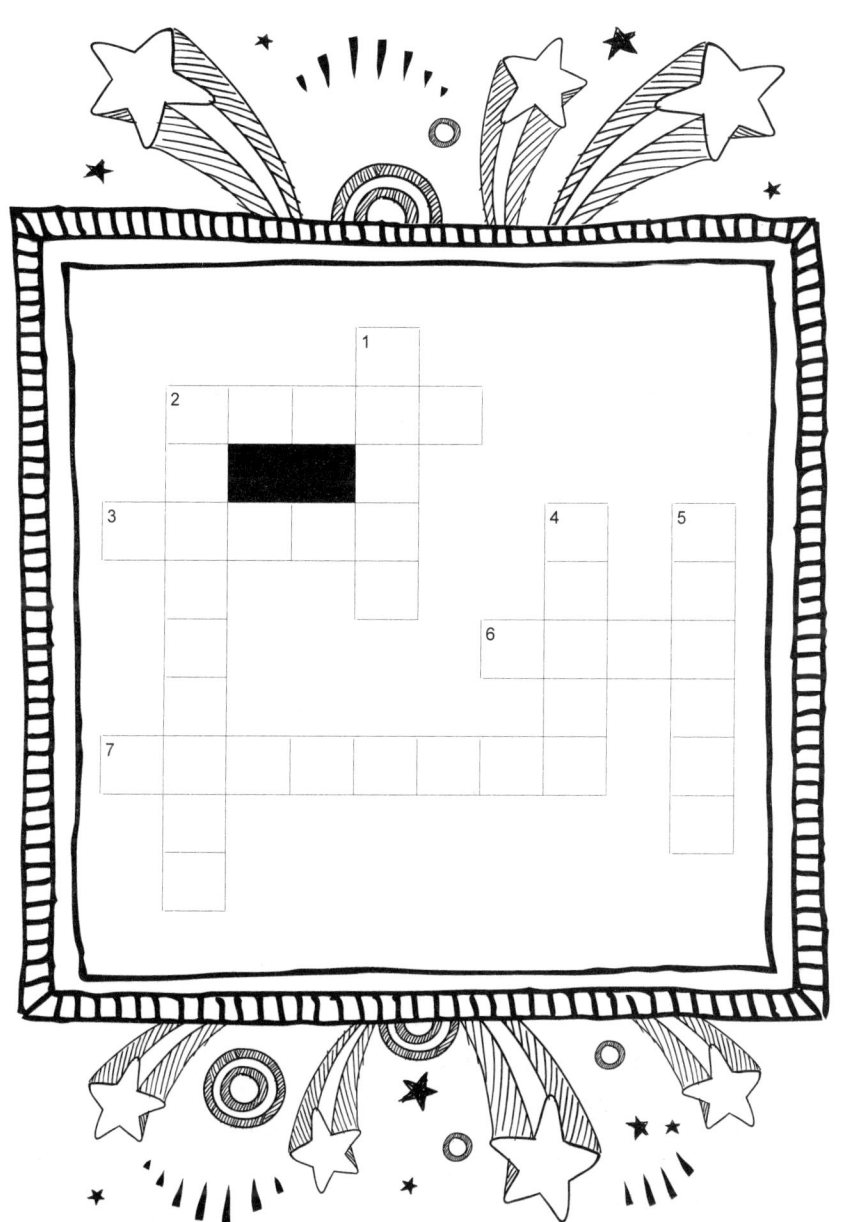

44. AN OLD MAN AND A BABY
LUKE 2:25-35

ACROSS

1. The old man wanted to see the Lord's what? (v. 26)

4. The old man was just and what else? (v. 25)

5. What the old man's eyes saw (v. 30)

7. The name of the old man (v. 25)

DOWN

2. How the old man knew he would not die until he saw baby Jesus (v. 26)

3. Why Jesus' parents brought Him to the temple (v. 27)

5. What the old man told Mary would be pierced (v. 35)

6. What the old man took baby Jesus into (v. 28)

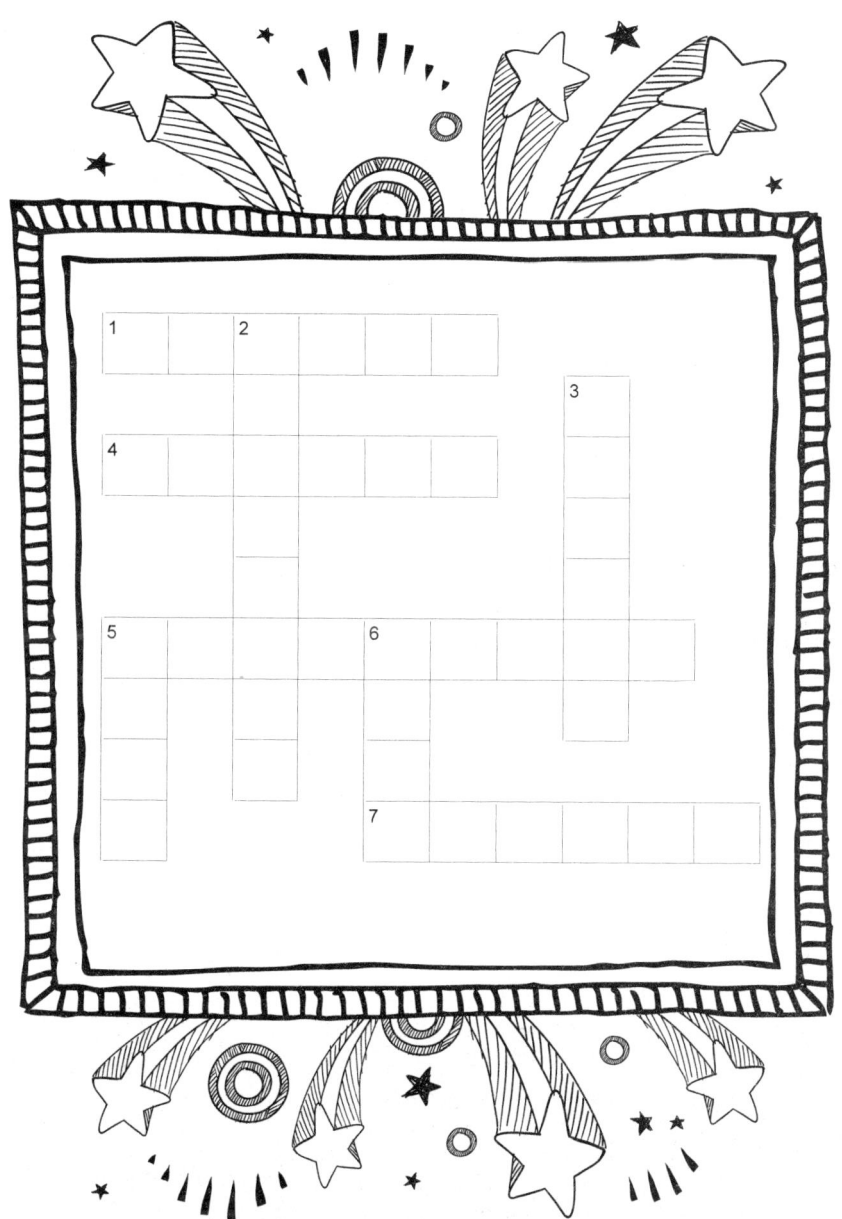

45. MORE VISITORS FOR YOUNG JESUS
MATTHEW 2:1-12

Now when **Jesus** was born in Bethlehem of Judaea in the days of Herod the king, behold, there came wise men from the east to Jerusalem, saying, Where is he that is **born** King of the Jews? for we have seen his **star** in the east, and are come to worship him. When Herod the king had heard these things, he was troubled, and all Jerusalem with him. And when he had gathered all the chief priests and scribes of the people together, he demanded of them where Christ should be born. And they said unto him, In **Bethlehem** of Judaea: for thus it is written by the prophet, And thou Bethlehem, in the land of Juda, art not the least among the princes of Juda: for out of thee shall come a Governor, that shall rule my people Israel. Then Herod, when he had privily called the wise men, enquired of them diligently what time the star appeared. And he sent them to Bethlehem, and said, Go and search diligently for the young child; and when ye have found him, bring me word again, that I may come and **worship** him also. When they had heard the **king**, they departed; and, lo, the star, which they saw in the **east**, went before them, till it came and stood over where the young child was. When they saw the star, they rejoiced with exceeding great joy. And when they were come into the house, they saw the young **child** with Mary his mother, and fell down, and worshipped him: and when they had opened their treasures, they presented unto him **gifts**; **gold**, and frankincense and **myrrh**. And being warned of God in a **dream** that they should not return to Herod, they departed into their own country another way.

46. Jesus Calls His First Disciples
LUKE 5:1–11

ACROSS

1. What Jesus promised the disciples would do (two words, v. 10)
4. Lake where Jesus called the disciples (v. 1)
5. Who Simon beckoned and signaled to (v. 7)
7. What the men were doing to their tools (v. 2)
8. Where Jesus told the men to take their boat (v. 4)

DOWN

2. These were breaking (v. 6)
3. What the men in one boat asked of the men in the other boat (v. 7)
6. What the miraculous catch of fish caused the boats to do (v. 7)
7. What the people wanted to hear from God (v. 1)

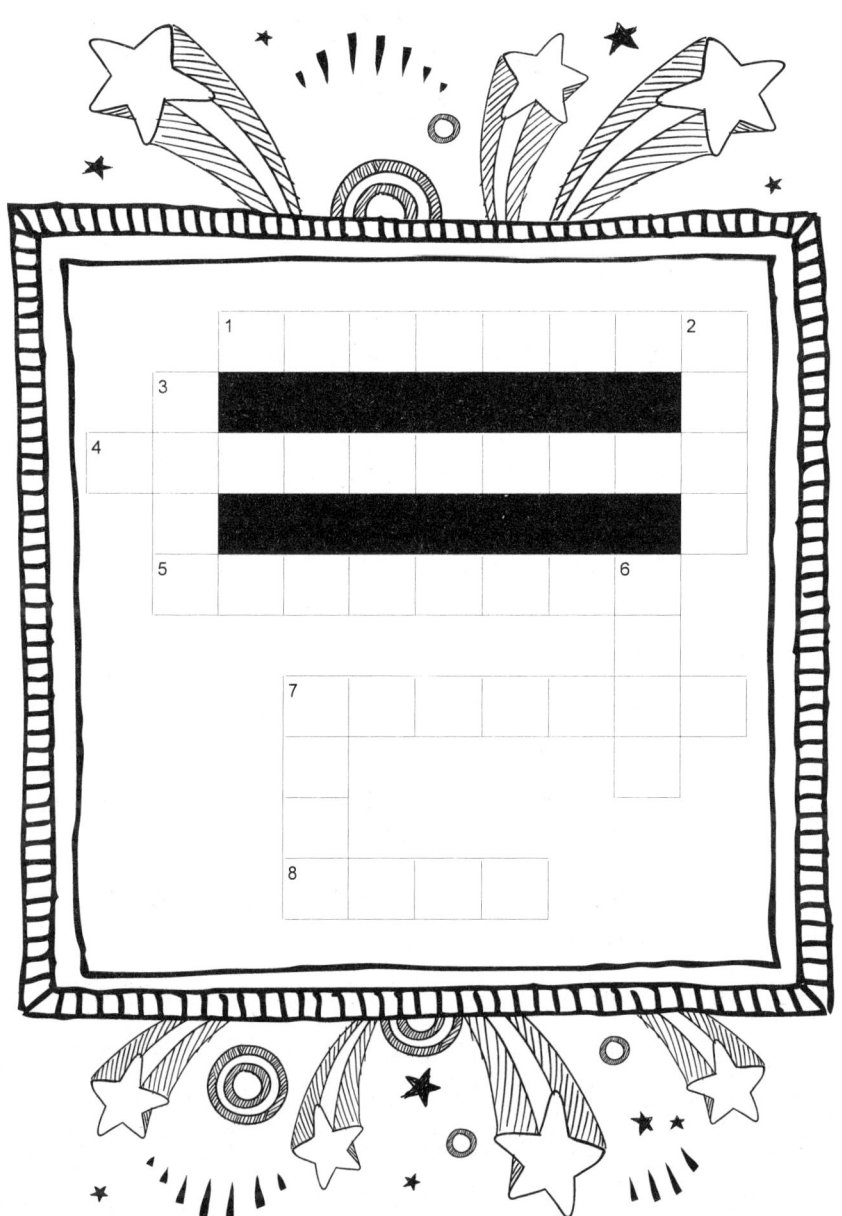

47. Jesus' First Miracle
JOHN 2:1-10

ACROSS

2. The ruler of the feast did this to a special drink (v. 9)

5. Jesus miraculously made this (v. 9)

6. Town where the wedding party took place (v. 1)

7. Large pots were made out of this material (v. 6)

DOWN

1. What liquid did Jesus start with? (v. 9)

3. Jesus' command after the miracle (v. 8)

4. Name of the region where the miracle occurred (v. 1)

7. Number of large pots (v. 6)

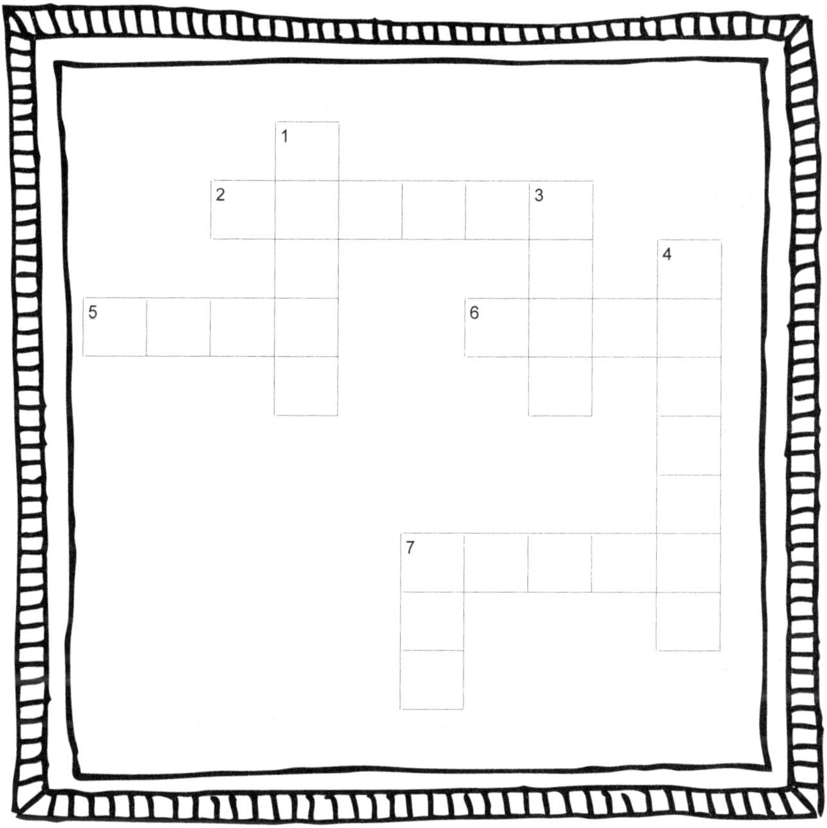

  **BONUS TRIVIA!**

What kind of seed did Jesus say the kingdom of heaven was like?

    a) dandelion
    b) mustard
    c) wheat
    d) apple

Answer: b) mustard (Mark 4:30–32)

48. ROCK VS. SAND
MATTHEW 7:24-27

Therefore whosoever **heareth** these sayings of mine, and **doeth** them, I will liken him unto a **wise** man, which **built** his house upon a **rock**: And the **rain** descended, and the **floods** came, and the winds blew, and beat upon that house; and it fell not: for it was founded upon a rock. And every one that heareth these sayings of mine, and doeth them not, shall be likened unto a **foolish** man, which built his **house** upon the **sand**: And the rain descended, and the floods came, and the **winds** blew, and beat upon that house; and it **fell**: and great was the fall of it.

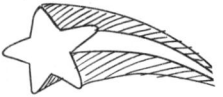 **BONUS TRIVIA!**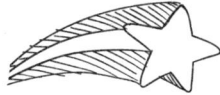

What were Egypt's kings called?

    a) satraps
    b) proconsuls
    c) pharaohs
    d) scary

Answer: c) pharaohs (Exodus 5:1-4)

49. SICK SERVANT MIRACULOUSLY HEALED
MATTHEW 8:5–13

And when Jesus was entered into **Capernaum**, there came unto him a **centurion**, beseeching him, and saying, Lord, my **servant** lieth at home **sick** of the palsy, grievously tormented. And Jesus saith unto him, I will come and **heal** him. The centurion answered and said, Lord, I am not worthy that thou shouldest come under my roof: but speak the **word** only, and my servant shall be healed. For I am a man under **authority**, having soldiers under me: and I say to this man, Go, and he goeth; and to another, Come, and he cometh; and to my servant, Do this, and he doeth it. When Jesus heard it, he marvelled, and said to them that followed, Verily I say unto you, I have not found so great **faith**, no, not in Israel. And I say unto you, That many shall come from the **east** and **west**, and shall sit down with Abraham, and Isaac, and Jacob, in the kingdom of heaven. But the children of the kingdom shall be cast out into outer darkness: there shall be weeping and gnashing of teeth. And Jesus said unto the centurion, Go thy way; and as thou hast **believed**, so be it done unto thee. And his servant was healed in the selfsame **hour**.

```
C A P E R N A U M B
E U J M N H Y T G E
N A B V T F H E A L
T I S I C K R E D I
U H A T C X W S W E
R F O Q A E Z O F V
I K R U S F V B R E
O L G T R T Y H N D
N O T N A V R E S A
P A U T H O R I T Y
```

50. DINNER WITH SINNERS
MATTHEW 9:9-13

And as Jesus passed forth from thence, he saw a man, named **Matthew**, **sitting** at the receipt of custom: and he saith unto him, <u>**Follow me**</u>. And he arose, and followed him. And it came to pass, as Jesus sat at meat in the **house**, behold, many publicans and sinners came and sat down with him and his disciples. And when the Pharisees saw it, they said unto his disciples, Why eateth your Master with publicans and **sinners**? But when **Jesus** heard that, he said unto them, They that be whole need not a physician, but they that are **sick**. But go ye and learn what that meaneth, I will have mercy, and not **sacrifice**: for I am not come to call the <u>**righteous**</u>, but sinners to repentance.

```
E M W O L L O F R S
S W S I N N E R S U
T A I J E S U S M O
F Y C V M O M S A E
D G K R S A R A T T
U O L M I S A S T H
V S R U O F R S H G
E S U O H X I W E I
B K J H G F D C W R
A S I T T I N G E S
```

BONUS TRIVIA!

Where did Jesus say we should store our treasure?

a) in heaven
b) in a bank
c) in a cave
d) in a pirate's chest

Answer: a) in heaven (Matthew 6:20)

51. THE DRAGNET
MATTHEW 13:47–50

Again, the kingdom of **heaven** is like unto a **net**, that was cast into the **sea**, and **gathered** of every kind: Which, when it was full, they drew to **shore**, and sat down, and gathered the **good** into vessels, but cast the **bad** away. So shall it be at the **end** of the world: the **angels** shall come forth, and sever the **wicked** from among the just, and shall cast them into the **furnace** of fire: there shall be wailing and gnashing of **teeth**.

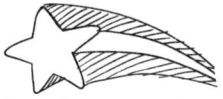 **BONUS TRIVIA!**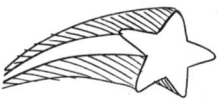

Why did Jesus use a whip to drive people out of the temple?

    a) They were making too much noise.
    b) They were using God's house as a marketplace.
    c) They were drinking wine.
    d) They were drawing pictures on their bulletins.

Answer: b) They were using God's house as a marketplace. (John 2:13–16)

52. WALKING ON WATER
MATTHEW 14:22-33

And straightway Jesus constrained his disciples to get into a ship, and to go before him unto the other side, while he sent the multitudes away. And when he had sent the multitudes away, he went up into a mountain apart to **pray**: and when the evening was come, he was there alone. But the ship was now in the midst of the sea, tossed with waves: for the **wind** was contrary. And in the **fourth** watch of the night Jesus went unto them, **walking** on the sea. And when the disciples saw him walking on the sea, they were troubled, saying, It is a spirit; and they cried out for **fear**. But straightway Jesus spake unto them, saying, Be of good cheer; it is I; be not afraid. And **Peter** answered him and said, **Lord**, if it be thou, bid me come unto thee on the water. And he said, **Come**. And when Peter was come down out of the ship, he walked on the water, to go to Jesus. But when he saw the wind boisterous, he was afraid; and beginning to **sink**, he cried, saying, Lord, <u>**save me**</u>. And immediately Jesus stretched forth his **hand**, and caught him, and said unto him, O thou of little faith, wherefore didst thou **doubt**? And when they were come into the ship, the wind ceased. Then they that were in the ship came and worshipped him, saying, Of a truth thou art the Son of God.

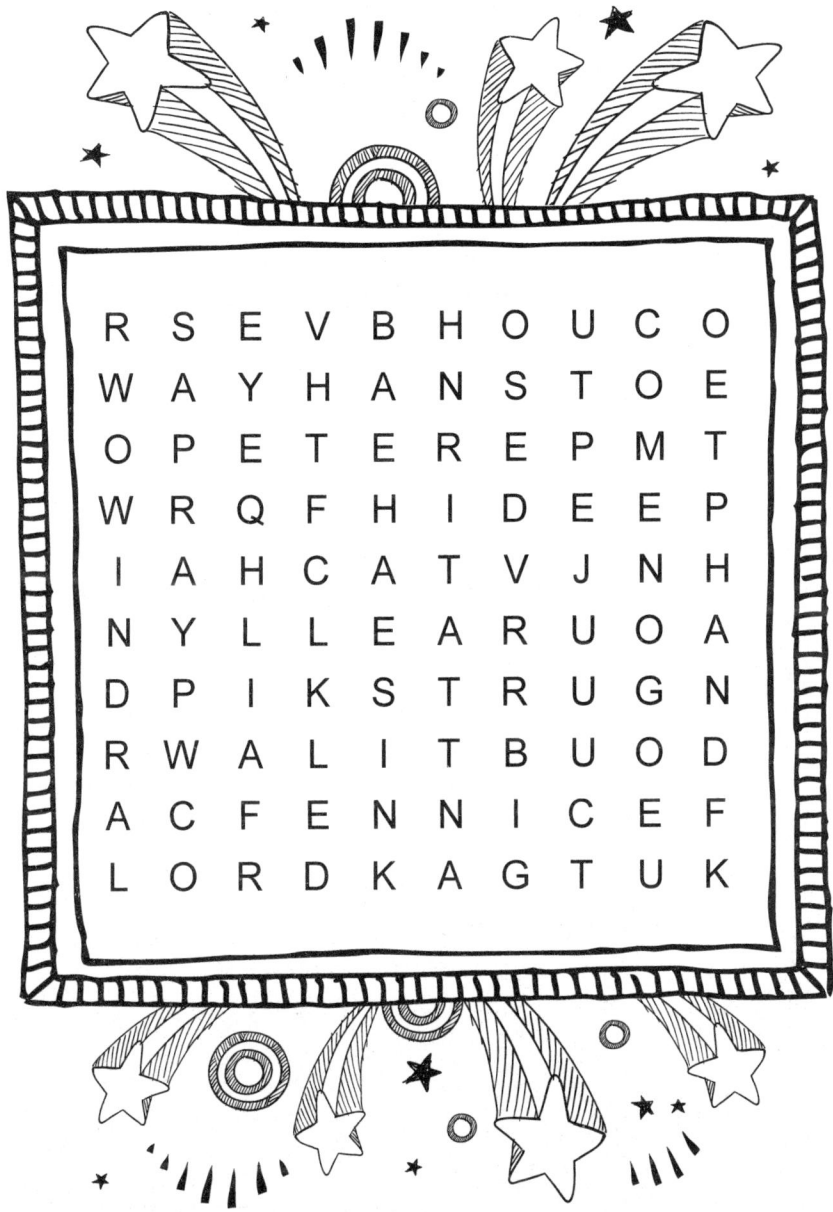

53. Friends Help a Man Find Healing
MARK 2:1-12

ACROSS

2. What Jesus saw in the men (v. 5)

3. City the miracle occurred in (v. 1)

6. What the friends broke through (v. 4)

8. The crowd blocked this (v. 2)

DOWN

1. One word in Jesus' conversation with the scribes (v. 9)

4. People's reaction when the paralyzed man walked (v. 12)

5. Why the men cut through the ceiling (two words, v. 2)

7. Number of people who carried the paralyzed man (v. 3)

54. The Four Soils
MARK 4:1–20

ACROSS

2. How fruit appeared on the good ground (two words, v. 8)

3. What a farmer does with seed (v. 3)

5. The plants that choked everything (v. 7)

7. What does the seed in this parable represent? (v. 14)

DOWN

1. What Jesus did with His parables (v. 2)

2. The sun did this to the plants (v. 6)

4. What the bad plants did to the new plants (v. 7)

6. One possible amount of return for each seed (v. 8)

55. THE GREAT STORM
MARK 4:35-41

And the same day, when the even was come, he saith unto them, Let us pass over unto the **other** side. And when they had sent away the multitude, they took him even as he was in the ship. And there were also with him other little ships. And there arose a great **storm** of **wind**, and the **waves** beat into the ship, so that it was now full. And he was in the hinder part of the ship, **asleep** on a **pillow**: and they awake him, and say unto him, Master, carest thou not that we perish? And he arose, and **rebuked** the wind, and said unto the **sea**, Peace, **be still**. And the wind ceased, and there was a great **calm**. And he said unto them, Why are ye so fearful? how is it that ye have **no faith**? And they feared exceedingly, and said one to another, What manner of man is this, that even the wind and the sea **obey** him?

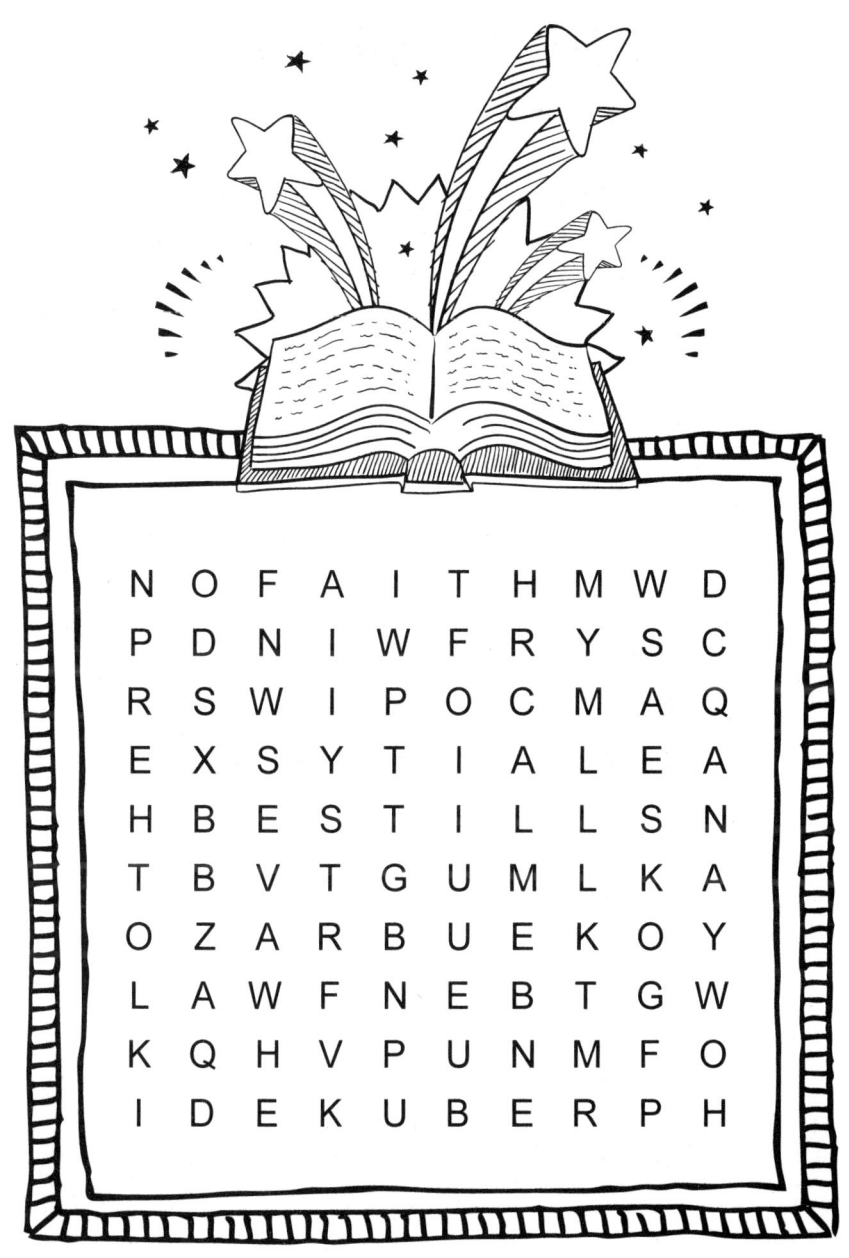

56. Demons Leave a Man to Enter Pigs
MARK 5:1-13

ACROSS

1. How many demons were in the man? (v. 9)

4. The name of the unclean spirit (v. 9)

6. What large number measured the pigs nearby? (v. 13)

7. The man cried out in a loud what? (v. 7)

DOWN

2. What did Jesus ask the man for? (v. 9)

3. Where, besides mountains, did the man live? (v. 5)

5. Name for a group of pigs (v. 13)

6. How many thousands of pigs were there? (v. 13)

57. MOUNTAINTOP TRANSFIGURATION
MARK 9:2-10

And after **six days** Jesus taketh with him Peter, and **James**, and **John**, and leadeth them up into an high mountain apart by themselves: and he was transfigured before them. And his raiment became shining, exceeding white as snow; so as no fuller on earth can white them. And there appeared unto them Elias with Moses: and they were **talking** with Jesus. And **Peter** answered and said to Jesus, Master, it is good for us to be here: and let us make three tabernacles; one for thee, and one for **Moses**, and one for Elias. For he wist not what to say; for they were sore afraid. And there was a **cloud** that overshadowed them: and a voice came out of the cloud, saying, This is my beloved Son: hear him. And suddenly, when they had looked round about, they saw no man any more, save Jesus only with themselves. And as they came down from the **mountain**, he charged them that they should tell no man what things they had seen, till the Son of man were **risen** from the dead. And they kept that saying with themselves, questioning one with another what the rising from the dead should mean.

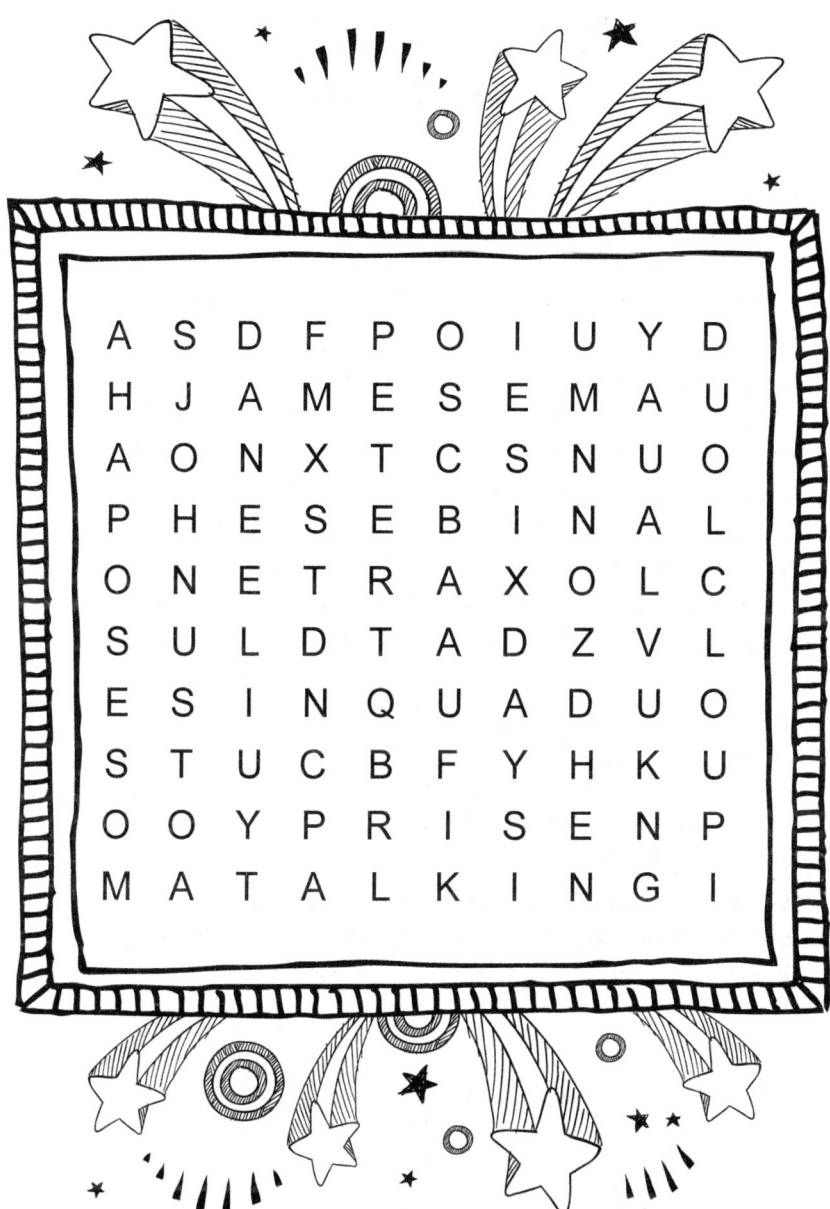

58. CHILDREN AND THE KINGDOM OF GOD
MARK 10:13-16

And they brought young **children** to him, that he should **touch** them: and his **disciples rebuked** those that brought them. But when **Jesus** saw it, he was much displeased, and said unto them, Suffer the **little** children to **come** unto me, and forbid them not: for of such is the kingdom of **God**. Verily I say unto you, Whosoever shall not receive the **kingdom** of God as a little **child**, he shall not enter therein. And he took them up in his **arms**, put his hands upon them, and **blessed** them.

```
C D E K U B E R E T
A U V C K L Z J O Y
C O M E T O U C H A
H B I T O D U D R T
W K I N G D O M C K
D L U J K I S G J O
E A T B L E S S E D
C H I L D R E N S N
D L I H C H I L U Y
D I S C I P L E S A
```

 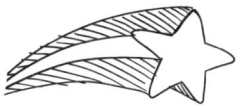

BONUS TRIVIA!

What were Peter and Andrew doing when Jesus asked them to be His disciples?

    a) playing chess
    b) building a house
    c) fishing
    d) cooking dinner

Answer: c) fishing (Matthew 4:18–19)

59. WHO CAN BE SAVED?
MARK 10:17–31

ACROSS

3. A large animal would go through this before a rich man would be saved (v. 25)

5. Who does God say will be first? (v. 31)

7. The group who heard this teaching (v. 23)

8. The person who taught (v. 27)

DOWN

1. Emotion of a rich young man (v. 22)

2. What the man wanted to do with eternal life (v. 17)

4. Animal used in this example (v. 25)

6. Who will really come in last (v. 31)

 **BONUS TRIVIA!**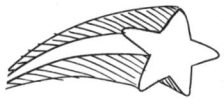

Who is Michael in the New Testament?

    a) an archangel
    b) a disciple of Jesus
    c) a Roman governor
    d) the author of Galatians

Answer: a) an archangel (Jude 9)

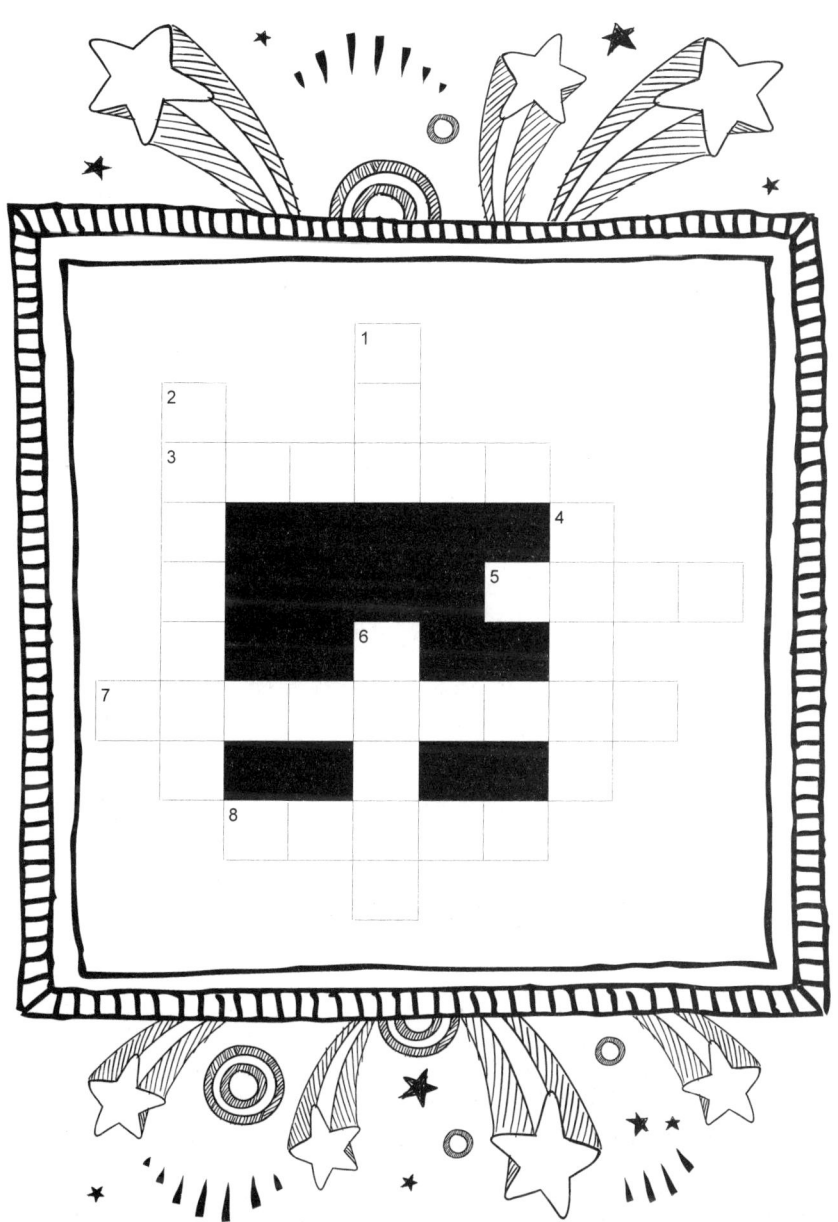

60. THE GOOD NEIGHBOR
LUKE 10:30–37

And Jesus answering said, A certain man went down from **Jerusalem** to **Jericho**, and fell among thieves, which stripped him of his raiment, and wounded him, and departed, leaving him **half dead**. And by chance there came down a certain **priest** that way: and when he saw him, he passed by on the **other** side. And likewise a **Levite**, when he was at the place, came and looked on him, and passed by on the other side. But a certain **Samaritan**, as he journeyed, came where he was: and when he saw him, he had compassion on him, and went to him, and bound up his **wounds**, pouring in **oil** and **wine**, and set him on his own beast, and brought him to an **inn**, and took care of him. And on the morrow when he departed, he took out two pence, and gave them to the host, and said unto him, Take care of him; and whatsoever thou spendest more, when I come again, I will repay thee. Which now of these three, thinkest thou, was neighbour unto him that fell among the thieves? And he said, He that shewed **mercy** on him. Then said Jesus unto him, Go, and do thou likewise.

61. A FOOLISH MAN
LUKE 12:13-21

ACROSS

2. Type of story Jesus told (v. 16)
3. Time period the fool thought he had laid up for (v. 19)
7. What one's life does not consist of (v. 15)
8. When God required the fool's soul (v. 20)

DOWN

1. The last in the list of things the fool planned to do (with "be," v. 19)
4. Type of man described in this Bible passage (v. 16)
5. What the fool wanted to tear down to build larger (v. 18)
6. Request for Jesus that led to this parable (v. 14)

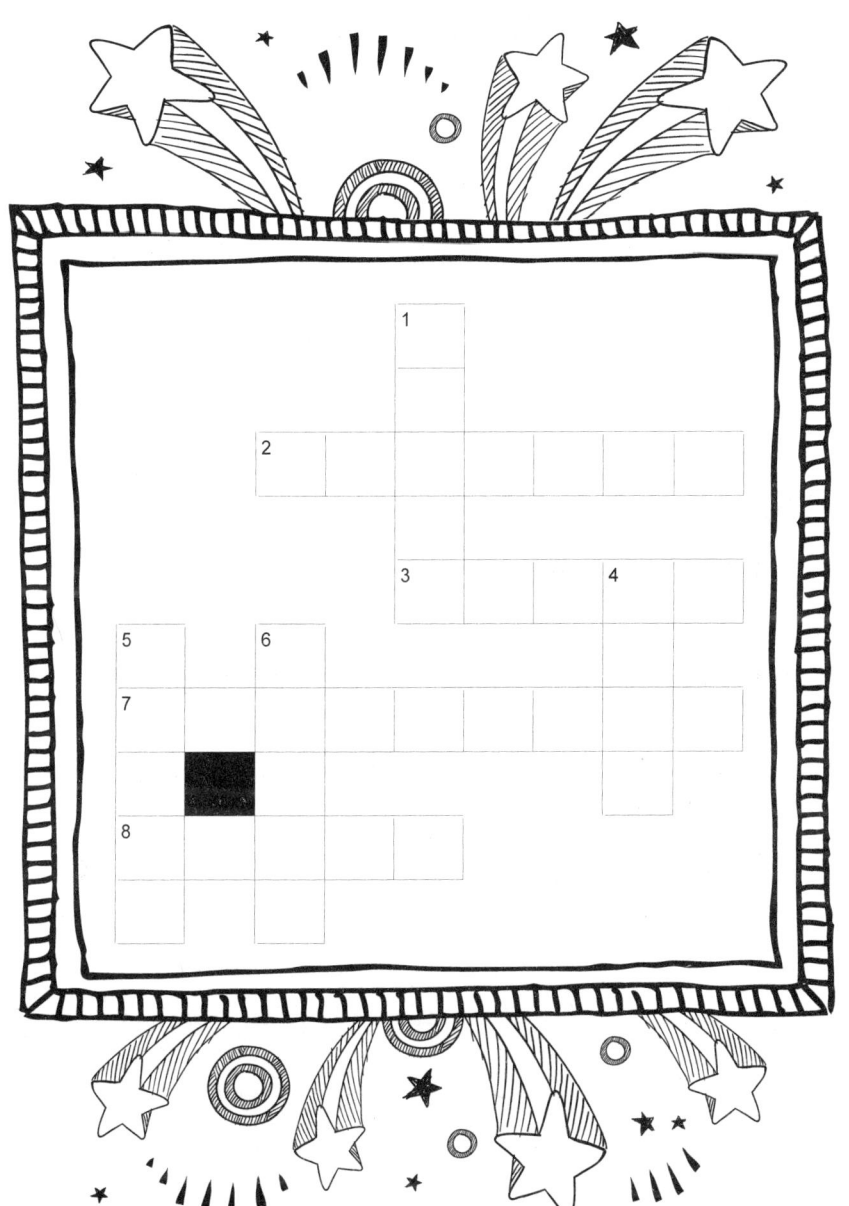

62. A PRODIGAL ("WASTEFUL") MAN
LUKE 15:11-24

ACROSS

3. The father had this toward his prodigal son (v. 20)

4. The second thing the father gave his returning son (v. 22)

6. The first thing the father gave his returning son (v. 22)

7. The returning son asked to be this type of servant (v. 19)

8. The father's servants had enough bread and this much more (with "to," v. 17)

DOWN

1. Which of the two sons was prodigal? (v. 12)

2. Who did the prodigal son join with in a far country? (v. 15)

5. Where did the prodigal son feed pigs? (v. 15)

63. PARABLE OF A RICH MAN AND A POOR MAN

LUKE 16:19–31

ACROSS

3. Place where the poor man was (v. 20)

6. Animals that licked the poor man's sores (v. 21)

8. Name of the poor man, in Abraham's bosom (v. 23)

9. What the rich man thought his brothers would do if someone appeared from the dead (v. 30)

DOWN

1. What the rich man received during his lifetime (v. 25)

2. What the poor man was (v. 20)

4. What the rich man wanted cooled (v. 24)

5. The rich man's family had Moses and who to persuade them? (v. 31)

7. Liquid the rich man requested (v. 24)

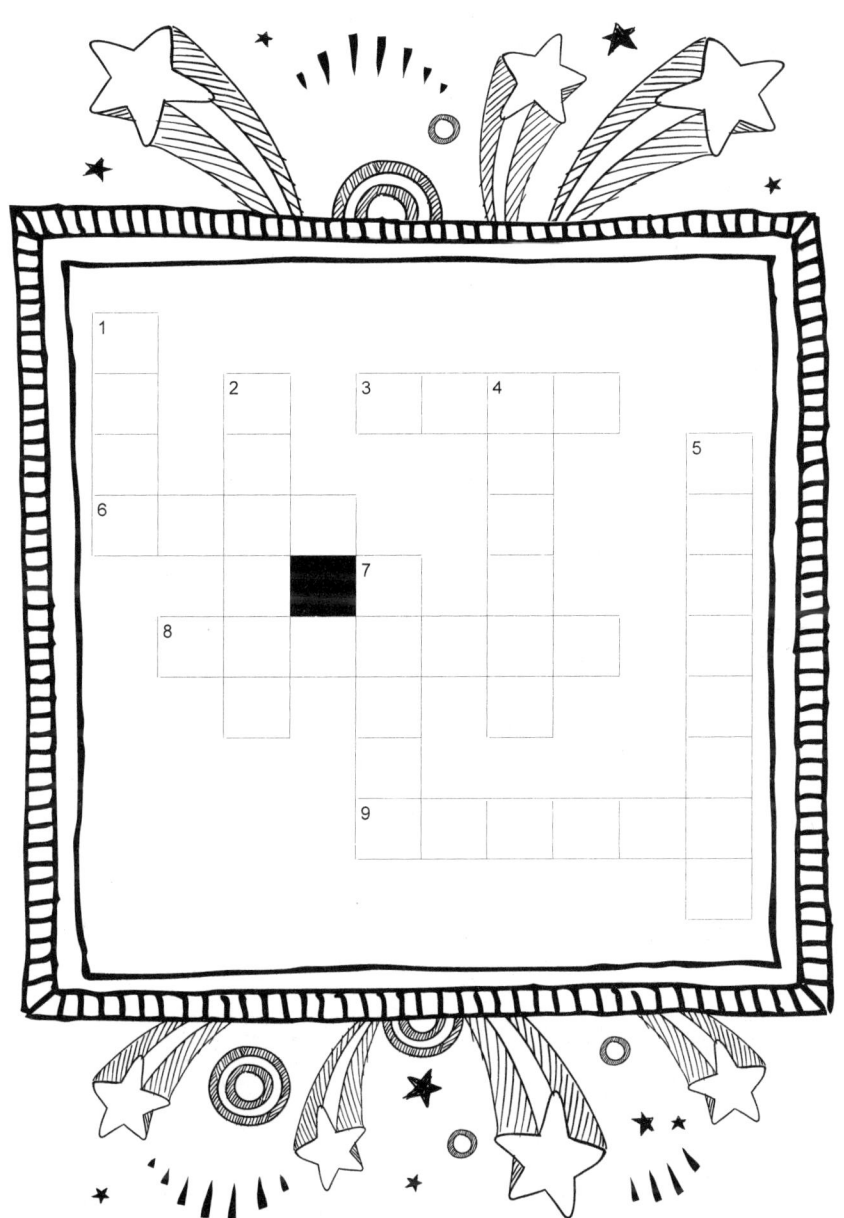

64. ONE THANKFUL AND NINE FORGETFUL LEPERS
LUKE 17:11–19

And it came to pass, as he went to **Jerusalem**, that he passed through the midst of **Samaria** and **Galilee**. And as he entered into a certain **village**, there met him **ten** men that were **lepers**, which stood afar off: And they lifted up their voices, and said, Jesus, Master, have mercy on us. And when he saw them, he said unto them, Go shew yourselves unto the priests. And it came to pass, that, as they went, they were **cleansed.** And **one** of them, when he saw that he was **healed**, turned back, and with a loud voice glorified God, and fell down on his face at his **feet**, giving him **thanks**: and he was a Samaritan. And Jesus answering said, Were there not ten cleansed? but where are the nine? There are not found that returned to give glory to God, save this stranger. And he said unto him, Arise, go thy way: thy **faith** hath made thee whole.

65. ZACCHAEUS
LUKE 19:1-10

And Jesus entered and passed through **Jericho**. And, behold, there was a man named **Zacchaeus**, which was the chief among the publicans, and he was rich. And he sought to see Jesus who he was; and could not for the press, because he was little of stature. And he ran before, and **climbed** up into a **sycomore** tree to see him: for he was to pass that way. And when Jesus came to the place, he looked **up**, and saw him, and said unto him, Zacchaeus, make haste, and come **down**; for to day I must abide at thy house. And he made haste, and came down, and received him joyfully. And when they saw it, they all murmured, saying, That he was gone to be guest with a man that is a **sinner**. And Zacchaeus stood, and said unto the Lord: Behold, Lord, the half of my goods I give to the **poor**; and if I have taken any thing from any man by false accusation, I restore him fourfold. And Jesus said unto him, This day is salvation come to this house, forsomuch as he also is a son of Abraham. For the Son of man is come to **seek** and to **save** that which was **lost**.

66. BORN TWICE
JOHN 3:1-8

There was a man of the **Pharisees**, named **Nicodemus**, a ruler of the Jews: The same came to Jesus by **night**, and said unto him, **Rabbi**, we know that thou art a teacher come from God: for no man can do these miracles that thou doest, except God be with him. Jesus answered and said unto him, Verily, verily, I say unto thee, Except a man be **<u>born again</u>**, he cannot see the kingdom of God. Nicodemus saith unto him, How can a man be born when he is **old**? can he enter the **second** time into his **mother's** womb, and be born? Jesus answered, Verily, verily, I say unto thee, Except a man be born of **water** and of the **Spirit**, he cannot enter into the kingdom of **God**. That which is born of the **flesh** is flesh; and that which is born of the Spirit is spirit. Marvel not that I said unto thee, Ye must be born again. The wind bloweth where it listeth, and thou hearest the sound thereof, but canst not tell whence it cometh, and whither it goeth: so is every one that is born of the Spirit.

67. FEEDING THE 5,000
JOHN 6:5-14

When Jesus then lifted up his eyes, and saw a great company come unto him, he saith unto **Philip**, Whence shall we buy **bread**, that these may eat? And this he said to prove him: for he himself knew what he would do. Philip answered him, Two hundred pennyworth of bread is not sufficient for them, that every one of them may take a little. One of his disciples, **Andrew**, Simon Peter's brother, saith unto him, There is a lad here, which hath **five** barley loaves, and **two** small fishes: but what are they among **so many**? And Jesus said, Make the men **sit** down. Now there was much grass in the place. So the men sat down, in number about five thousand. And Jesus took the loaves; and when he had given **thanks**, he distributed to the disciples, and the disciples to them that were set down; and likewise of the fishes as much as they would. When they were filled, he said unto his disciples, **Gather** up the fragments that remain, that nothing be lost. Therefore they gathered them together, and filled **twelve baskets** with the fragments of the five **barley** loaves, which remained over and above unto them that had eaten. Then those men, when they had seen the miracle that Jesus did, said, This is of a truth that prophet that should come into the world.

68. A BLIND MAN SEES
JOHN 9:1-11

And as Jesus passed by, he saw a man which was **blind** from his **birth**. And his disciples asked him, saying, Master, who did sin, this man, or his parents, that he was born blind? Jesus answered, Neither hath this man sinned, nor his parents: but that the works of God should be made manifest in him. I must work the works of him that sent me, while it is day: the night cometh, when no man can work. As long as I am in the world, I am the light of the world. When he had thus spoken, he spat on the **ground**, and made clay of the spittle, and he anointed the **eyes** of the blind man with the clay, And said unto him, Go, **wash** in the **pool** of **Siloam**, (which is by interpretation, **Sent**.) He went his way therefore, and washed, and came **seeing**. The neighbours therefore, and they which before had seen him that he was blind, said, Is not this he that sat and begged? Some said, This is he: others said, He is like him: but he said, I am he. Therefore said they unto him, How were thine eyes **opened**? He answered and said, A man that is called Jesus made clay, and anointed mine eyes, and said unto me, Go to the pool of Siloam, and wash: and I went and washed, and I received sight.

69. Jesus Raises a Friend from the Dead
JOHN 11:14-44

ACROSS

1. Jesus called Himself the resurrection and what else? (v. 25)
5. Name of the dead man (v. 14)
6. Place where the grave was (v. 38)
8. "Thy brother shall rise _____" (v. 23)
9. What is seen if one believes (v. 40)

DOWN

2. Number of days the man was dead (v. 39)
3. The command Jesus gave for the stone: "_____ ye _____" (v. 39)
4. What Jesus saw people doing (v. 33)

70. A Powerful Example
JOHN 13:1-14

ACROSS

2. What the Teacher poured water into (v. 5)
3. Part of the disciples that the Teacher washed (v. 5)
4. Name of the man who would betray the Teacher (v. 2)
6. Name of the feast in this Bible passage (v. 1)

DOWN

1. Cloth the Teacher used in this example (v. 4)
2. What Judas planned to do to the Teacher (v. 2)
4. The person who set this example (v. 8)
5. Who entered the heart of Judas Iscariot? (v. 2)

71. Jesus Comforts His Troubled Disciples
JOHN 14:1–7

Let not your **heart** be **troubled**: ye believe in God, believe also in me. In my **Father's** house are many mansions: if it were not so, I would have told you. I go to **prepare** a **place** for you. And if I go and prepare a place for you, I will **come** again, and **receive** you unto myself; that where I am, there ye may be also. And whither I go ye know, and the way ye know. **Thomas** saith unto him, Lord, we know not whither thou goest; and how can we know the way? Jesus saith unto him, I am the **way**, the **truth**, and the **life**: no man cometh unto the Father, but by **me**. If ye had known me, ye should have known my Father also: and from henceforth ye know him, and have seen him.

```
R E C E I V E S A T
A T P H E A R T I E
W E R T Y E U I O P
T R E U H T I W A Y
M K P T T G F D S A
E J A B H H C Q L I
E F R O O O M I E
T E E Y H T M N F F
U W P L A C E A E E
D E L B U O R T S B
```

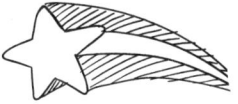 

BONUS TRIVIA!

What king was known around the world for his wisdom?

    a) Solomon
    b) Nebuchadnezzar
    c) Agrippa
    d) Burger King

Answer: a) Solomon (1 Kings 4:29)

72. PALM SUNDAY
MARK 11:1-11

And when they came nigh to **Jerusalem**, unto Bethphage and **Bethany**, at the mount of **Olives**, he sendeth forth **two** of his disciples, And saith unto them, Go your way into the **village** over against you: and as soon as ye be entered into it, ye shall find a colt tied, whereon never man sat; loose him, and bring him. And if any man say unto you, Why do ye this? say ye that the Lord hath need of him; and straightway he will send him hither. And they went their way, and found the **colt** tied by the door without in a place where two ways met; and they loose him. And certain of them that stood there said unto them, What do ye, loosing the colt? And they said unto them even as Jesus had commanded: and they let them go. And they brought the colt to Jesus, and cast their garments on him; and he sat upon him. And many spread their garments in the way: and others cut down **branches** off the trees, and strawed them in the way. And they that went before, and they that followed, cried, saying, **Hosanna**; Blessed is he that cometh in the name of the Lord: Blessed be the kingdom of our father David, that cometh in the name of the Lord: Hosanna in the highest. And Jesus entered into Jerusalem, and into the **temple**: and when he had **looked** round about upon all things, and now the eventide was come, he went out unto Bethany with the twelve.

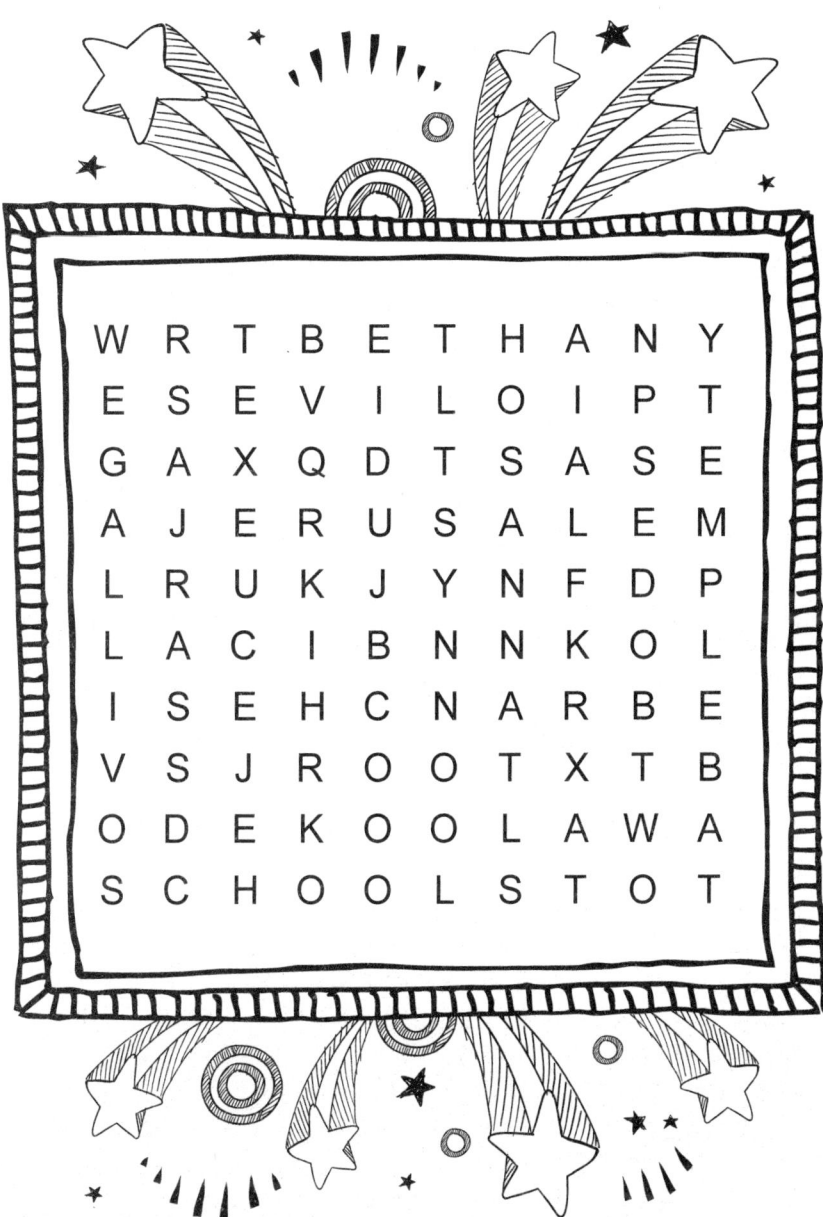

73. THE LORD'S SUPPER
MARK 14:12-16, 18-26

And the first day of **unleavened** bread, when they killed the passover, his disciples said unto him, Where wilt thou that we go and prepare that thou mayest eat the passover? And he sendeth forth two of his disciples, and saith unto them, Go ye into the **city**, and there shall meet you a man bearing a pitcher of **water**: **follow** him. And wheresoever he shall go in, say ye to the goodman of the house, The Master saith, Where is the guestchamber, where I shall eat the passover with my disciples? And he will shew you a large **upper room** furnished and prepared: there make ready for us. And his disciples went forth, and came into the city, and found as he had said unto them: and they made ready the **passover**. . . . And as they sat and did eat, Jesus said, Verily I say unto you, One of you which eateth with me shall **betray** me. And they began to be sorrowful, and to say unto him one by one, Is it I? and another said, Is it I? And he answered and said unto them, It is one of the twelve, that dippeth with me in the dish. The Son of man indeed goeth, as it is written of him: but woe to that man by whom the Son of man is betrayed! good were it for that man if he had never been born. And as they did eat, Jesus took **bread**, and blessed, and brake it, and gave to them, and said, Take, eat: this is **my body**. And he took the **cup**, and when he had given thanks, he gave it to them: and they all drank of it. And he said unto them, This is **my blood** of the new testament, which is shed for many. Verily I say unto you, I will drink no more of the fruit of the vine, until that day that I drink it new in the kingdom of God. And when they had sung an **hymn**, they went out into the mount of Olives.

74. Garden of Gethsemane
LUKE 22:39-46

And he came out, and went, as he was wont, to the **mount** of **Olives**; and his disciples also followed him. And when he was at the place, he said unto them, Pray that ye enter not into temptation. And he was withdrawn from them about a stone's cast, and kneeled down, and **prayed**, saying, Father, if thou be willing, remove this cup from me: nevertheless <u>**not my will**</u>, but thine, be done. And there appeared an **angel** unto him from heaven, strengthening him. And being in an agony he prayed more earnestly: and his **sweat** was as it were great **drops** of **blood** falling down to the **ground**. And when he rose up from prayer, and was come to his disciples, he found them sleeping for **sorrow**, And said unto them, Why sleep ye? rise and pray, lest ye enter into temptation.

75. HEARING PROBLEMS
LUKE 22:47-53

And while he yet spake, behold a multitude, and he that was called **Judas**, one of the twelve, went before them, and drew near unto Jesus to kiss him. But Jesus said unto him, Judas, **betrayest** thou the Son of man with a **kiss**? When they which were about him saw what would follow, they said unto him, Lord, shall we smite with the **sword**? And one of them smote the **servant** of the high priest, and <u>**cut off**</u> his right **ear**. And Jesus answered and said, Suffer ye thus far. And he touched his ear, and **healed** him. Then Jesus said unto the chief priests, and captains of the temple, and the elders, which were come to him, Be ye come out, as against a thief, with swords and staves? When I was **daily** with you in the **temple**, ye stretched forth no hands against me: but this is your **hour**, and the power of **darkness**.

```
O H E A L E D P S B
E O D E P T U H E C
T U A I K S E T R C
E R R Y N I R A V U
M U K I L A S T A T
P Q N A Y I G S N O
L I E E Q E A A T F
E N S W U A R D O F
Q T S W O R D U W H
B A S D F G H J K L
```

 **BONUS TRIVIA!**

What did God put in the sky as a promise never again to destroy the earth with a flood?

  a) birds
  b) the moon
  c) a rainbow
  d) the space shuttle

Answer: c) a rainbow (Genesis 9:13–16)

76. A ROOSTER CROWS
MATTHEW 26:69-75

Now **Peter** sat without in the palace: and a damsel came unto him, saying, Thou also wast with Jesus of **Galilee**. But he **denied** before them all, saying, I know not what thou sayest. And when he was gone out into the porch, another maid saw him, and said unto them that were there, This fellow was also with Jesus of **Nazareth**. And **again** he denied with an **oath**, I do not know the man. And after a while came unto him they that stood by, and said to Peter, Surely thou also art one of them; for thy speech bewrayeth thee. Then began he to curse and to swear, saying, I know not the man. And immediately the cock crew. And Peter **remembered** the **word** of Jesus, which said unto him, Before the cock **crow**, thou shalt deny me thrice. And he went out, and **wept** bitterly.

```
R E M E M B E R E D
H A N M X E V R E M
T T D R O W E P T P
A C E Q O I U Y T E
O P S R A S D F G T
R A C G A L I L E E
E G H A T Z Y X W R
J A B C Y E A J I V
A I V U D E I N E D
M N B V C X Z L K J
```

BONUS TRIVIA!

How did Jesus calm a storm on the sea?

  a) He spoke to the storm.
  b) He touched the water with a stick.
  c) He waved His arms over the sea.
  d) He dipped His robe into the water.

Answer: a) He spoke to the storm. (Mark 4:39)

77. BARABBAS GETS FREEDOM— JESUS GETS DEATH
MARK 15:6–14

Now at that feast he released unto them one **prisoner**, whomsoever they desired. And there was one named **Barabbas**, which lay bound with them that had made insurrection with him, who had committed **murder** in the insurrection. And the multitude crying aloud began to desire him to do as he had ever done unto them. But **Pilate** answered them, saying, Will ye that I release unto you the **King** of the **Jews**? For he knew that the **chief** priests had delivered him for **envy**. But the chief priests moved the people, that he should rather **release** Barabbas unto them. And Pilate answered and said again unto them, What will ye then that I shall do unto him whom ye call the King of the Jews? And they cried out again, Crucify him. Then Pilate said unto them, Why, what evil hath he done? And they cried out the more exceedingly, **Crucify** him.

78. JESUS KILLED!
JOHN 19:17-27

ACROSS

2. Jesus said Mary would now be this to His favorite disciple (v. 27)

4. Hebrew word for place where Jesus was killed (v. 17)

5. What was done to Jesus and others (v. 18)

7. "The place of a _____" (v. 17)

8. One of the three languages on the sign on Jesus' cross (v. 20)

DOWN

1. The person who wrote the sign on the cross (v. 19)

3. Number of criminals killed along with Jesus (v. 18)

6. How many parts did the soldiers divide Jesus' garments into? (v. 23)

7. Jesus said His favorite disciple would now be this to Mary (v. 26)

79. Jesus Buried
JOHN 19:38–42

And after this **Joseph** of Arimathaea, being a **disciple** of Jesus, but **secretly** for fear of the Jews, besought Pilate that he might take away the body of Jesus: and Pilate gave him leave. He came therefore, and took the body of Jesus. And there came also **Nicodemus**, which at the first came to Jesus by **night**, and brought a **mixture** of **myrrh** and **aloes**, about an hundred pound weight. Then took they the **body** of Jesus, and wound it in linen clothes with the **spices**, as the manner of the Jews is to bury. Now in the place where he was crucified there was a **garden**; and in the garden a **new** sepulchre, wherein was never man yet laid. There laid they Jesus therefore because of the Jews' preparation day; for the sepulchre was nigh at hand.

80. Resurrection!
LUKE 24:1-9

Now upon the **first** day of the week, <u>**very early**</u> in the **morning**, they came unto the sepulchre, bringing the spices which they had prepared, and certain others with them. And they found the **stone** rolled **away** from the sepulchre. And they entered in, and found not the body of the Lord Jesus. And it came to pass, as they were much perplexed thereabout, behold, two men stood by them in shining garments: And as they were afraid, and bowed down their faces to the earth, they said unto them, Why seek ye the **living** among the **dead**? He is **not** here, but <u>**is risen**</u>: remember how he spake unto you when he was yet in Galilee, saying, The Son of man must be delivered into the hands of sinful men, and be crucified, and the **third** day rise **again**. And they remembered his words, and returned from the sepulchre, and told all these things unto the **eleven**, and to all the rest.

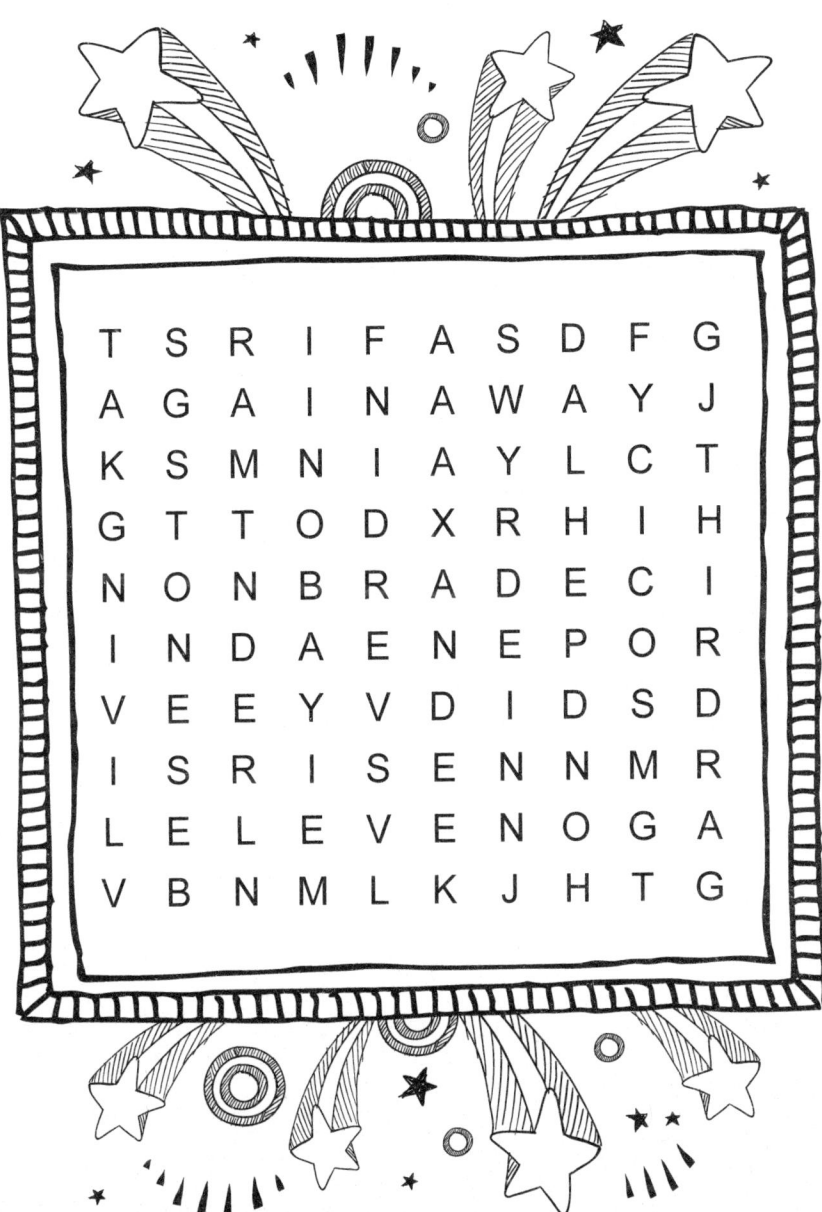

81. THOMAS DOUBTS
JOHN 20:24-29

But Thomas, one of the **twelve**, called **Didymus**, was not with them when Jesus came. The other disciples therefore said unto him, We have seen the L0RD. But he said unto them, Except I shall see in his **hands** the print of the nails, and put my **finger** into the print of the nails, and thrust my hand into his side, I will **not believe**. And after eight days again his disciples were within, and Thomas with them: then came Jesus, the **doors** being shut, and stood in the midst, and said, **Peace** be unto you. Then saith he to Thomas, Reach hither thy finger, and behold my hands; and reach hither thy hand, and thrust it into my **side**: and be not **faithless**, but believing. And Thomas answered and said unto him, My L0RD and my God. Jesus saith unto him, **Thomas**, because thou hast seen me, thou hast believed: **blessed** are they that have not seen, and yet have believed.

```
T I J L O R D U N E
S W B L E S S E D V
P U E G H A N D S E
X E N L L R V T I I
C I A O V S B H D L
F H N C R E T O E E
T B M O E X Y M E B
Y V O K P W N A C T
G D I D Y M U S N O
S S E L H T I A F N
```

 **BONUS TRIVIA!**

What did the mother of James and John once ask Jesus?

    a) that her sons would never die

    b) that her sons could sit at Jesus' side in heaven

    c) that her sons could turn stones into gold

    d) that her sons would have many children

Answer: b) that her sons could sit at Jesus' side in heaven (Matthew 20:21)

82. ASCENSION
ACTS 1:3-11

To whom also he shewed himself alive after his passion by many infallible proofs, being seen of them **forty** days, and speaking of the things pertaining to the kingdom of God: And, being assembled together with them, commanded them that they should not depart from Jerusalem, but wait for the promise of the Father, which, saith he, ye have heard of me. For John truly baptized with water; but ye shall be **baptized** with the Holy Ghost not many days hence. When they therefore were come together, they asked of him, saying, Lord, wilt thou at this time restore again the kingdom to Israel? And he said unto them, It is not for you to know the times or the seasons, which the Father hath put in his own **power**. But ye shall receive power, after that the Holy Ghost is come upon you: and ye shall be witnesses unto me both in Jerusalem, and in all Judaea, and in Samaria, and unto the uttermost part of the earth. And when he had spoken these things, while they beheld, he was taken up; and a **cloud** received him out of their **sight**. And while they looked stedfastly toward heaven as he went up, behold, **two** men stood by them in **white** apparel; Which also said, Ye men of **Galilee**, why stand ye gazing up into heaven? this <u>**same Jesus**</u>, which is <u>**taken up**</u> from you into heaven, shall so **come** in like manner as ye have seen him go into heaven.

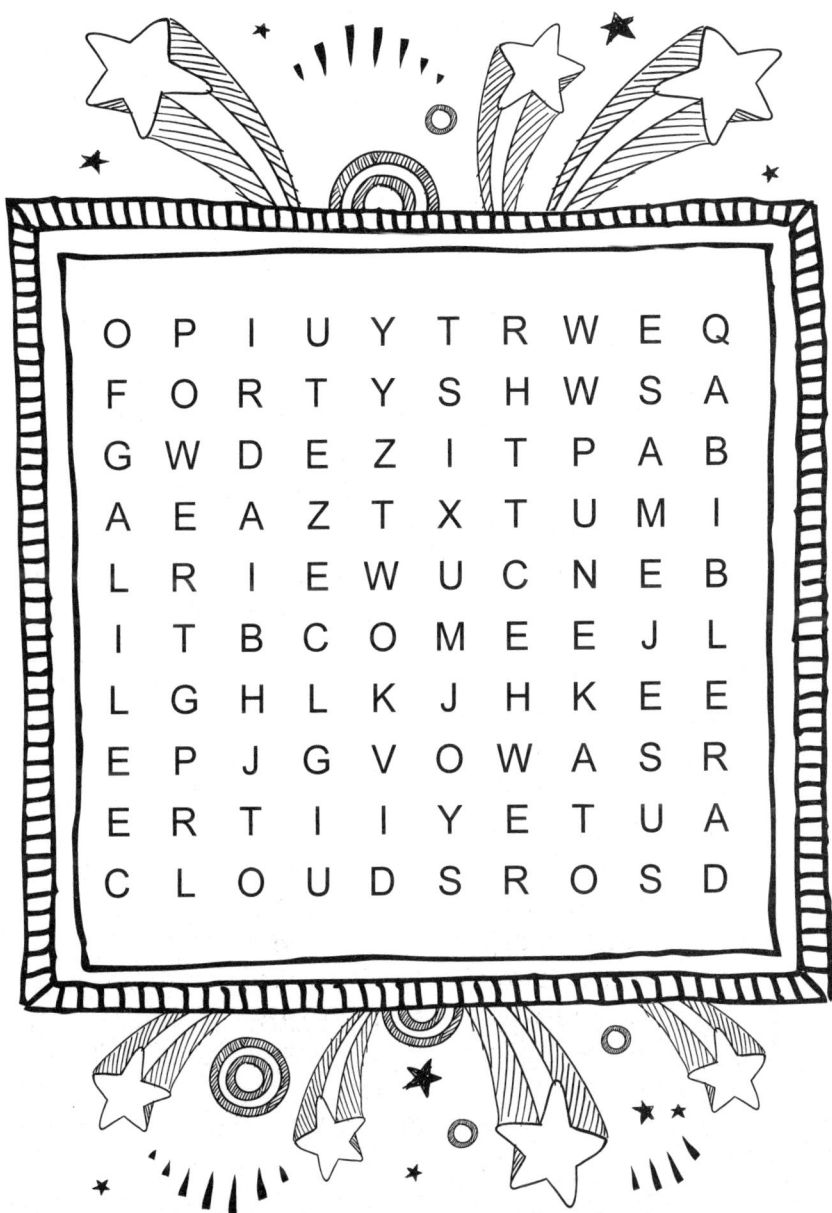

83. THE BIRTH OF THE CHURCH
ACTS 2:1-8

ACROSS

2. What the believers thought they heard (v. 2)

3. The special day the believers were together (v. 1)

6. This came from heaven (v. 2)

8. How the event occurred (v. 2)

9. Who enabled the believers to speak in other languages? (v. 4)

DOWN

1. What appeared above each of the believers? (v. 3)

4. "And there appeared unto them cloven _____" (v. 3)

5. In whose tongue and language did each person hear? (v. 6)

6. The first thing the believers did when filled with the Holy Ghost (v. 4)

7. How many were filled with the Holy Ghost? (v. 4)

84. MIGHTY JESUS
REVELATION 19:11–16

And I saw **heaven** opened, and behold a **white horse**; and he that sat upon him was called **Faithful** and True, and in righteousness he doth **judge** and make war. His eyes were as a flame of fire, and on his head were many **crowns**; and he had a name written, that no man knew, but he himself. And he was clothed with a vesture dipped in **blood**: and his name is called The **Word of God**. And the **armies** which were in heaven followed him upon white horses, clothed in fine linen, white and **clean**. And out of his mouth goeth a sharp **sword**, that with it he should smite the nations: and he shall **rule** them with a rod of iron: and he treadeth the winepress of the fierceness and **wrath** of Almighty God. And he hath on his vesture and on his thigh a name written, KING OF KINGS, AND **LORD** OF LORDS.

ANSWERS

1

2

3
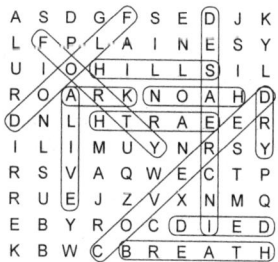

4
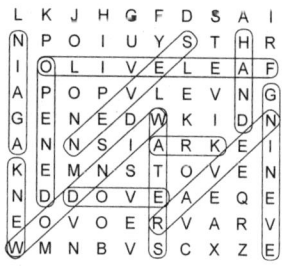

5
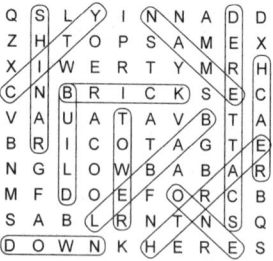

6

7

8

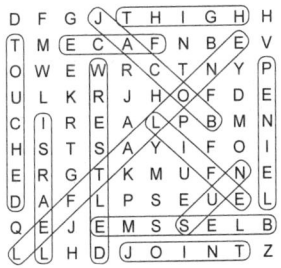

9

10

11

12

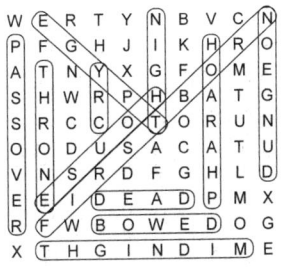

13

14

15
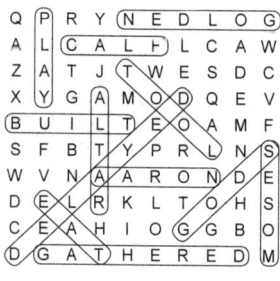

16
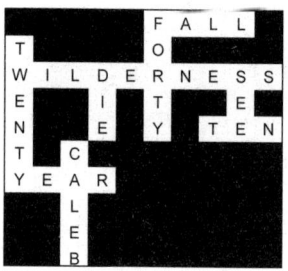

17
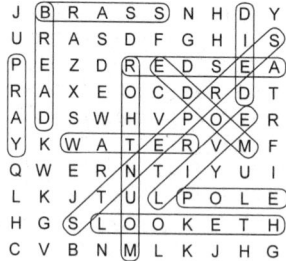

18
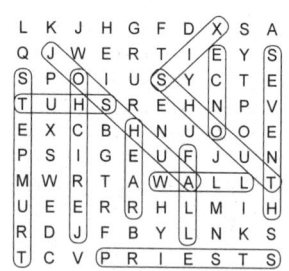

19
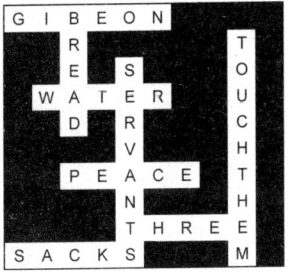

20

21
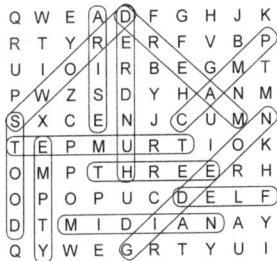

22
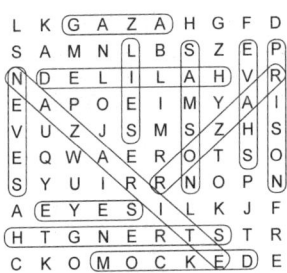

23

24
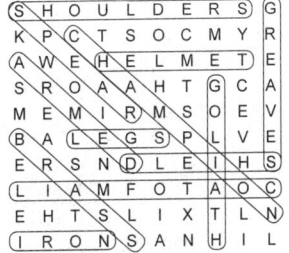

25

26

27

28
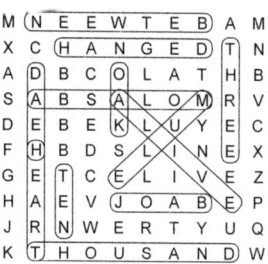

29

30
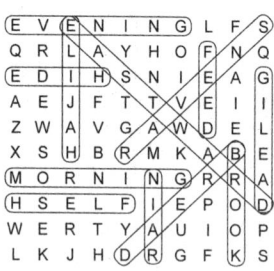

31

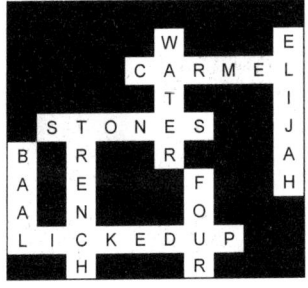

32

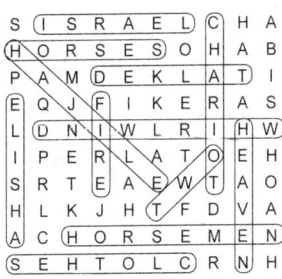

33

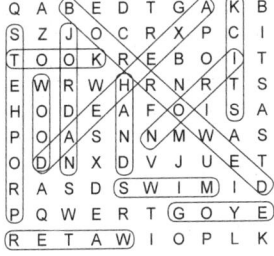

34

| N O T H I N G O N G |
| K J H G F S D A K O |
| H E Z E R K A I D L |
| B A B Y L O N I R D |
| K A U S V G L M A O |
| C T H A I K E Z E H |
| I X G U S L E A H K |
| S P I C E S V U B R |
| S D E L E T T E R S |
| R T E H P O R P R E |

35

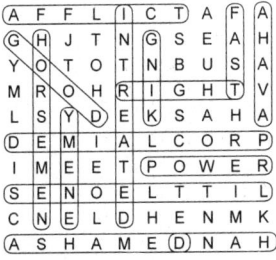

36

| D O G F O E S U O H |
| E P R O P H E C Y B |
| V S N H O A S E R D |
| I A H U P K M E I E |
| E H S U R J E C L R |
| C E I O T L R P N I |
| R O W S F U M I E H |
| E V I L R E P O R T |
| P T A S T K A T C S |
| A F R A I D S R K L |

37
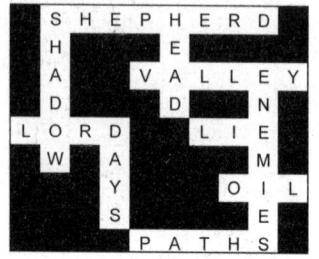

38
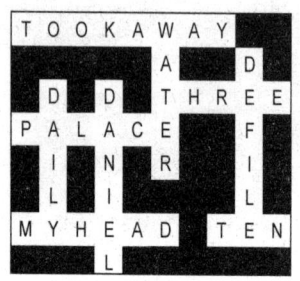

39

40
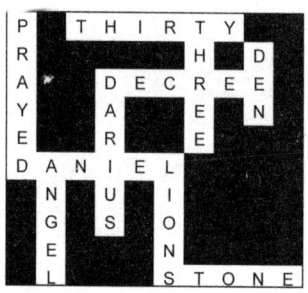

41

42
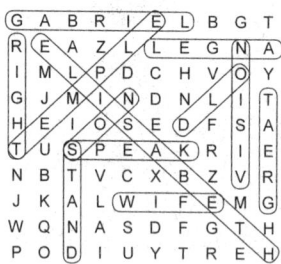

43

44

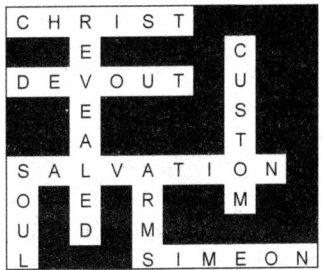

45

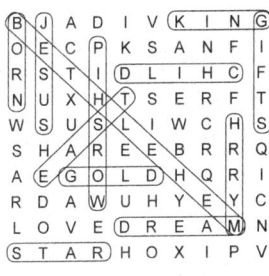

46

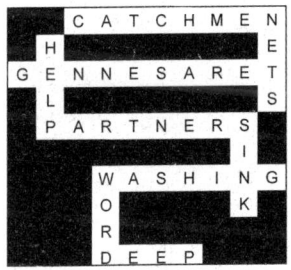

47

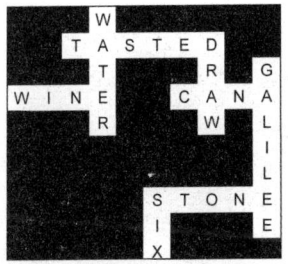

48

49
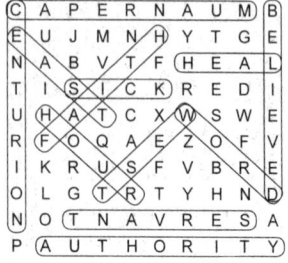

50
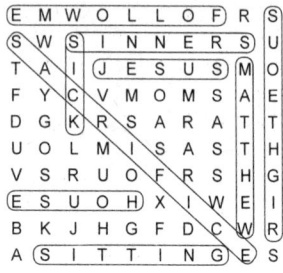

51

52

53
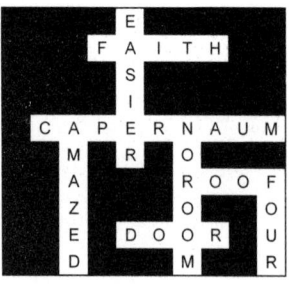

54
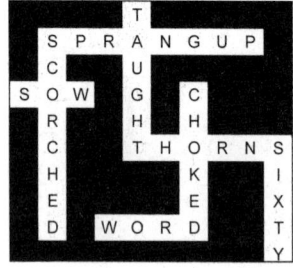

55

56
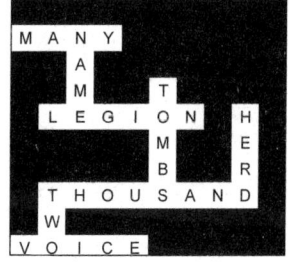

57

58

59

60

61

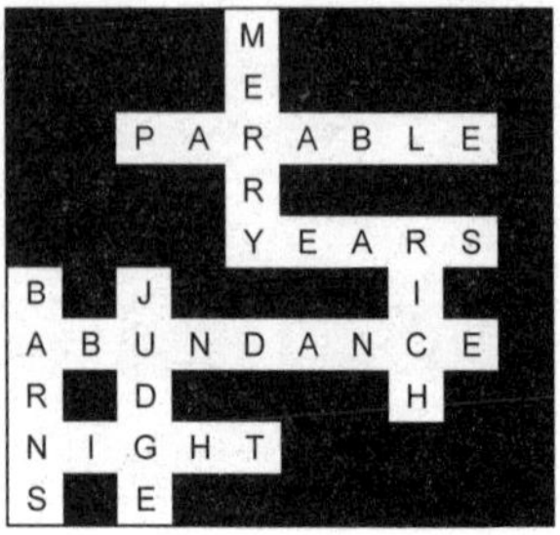
MERCY
PARABLE
YEARS
BARNS
JUDGE
ABUNDANCE
RICH
NIGHT

62

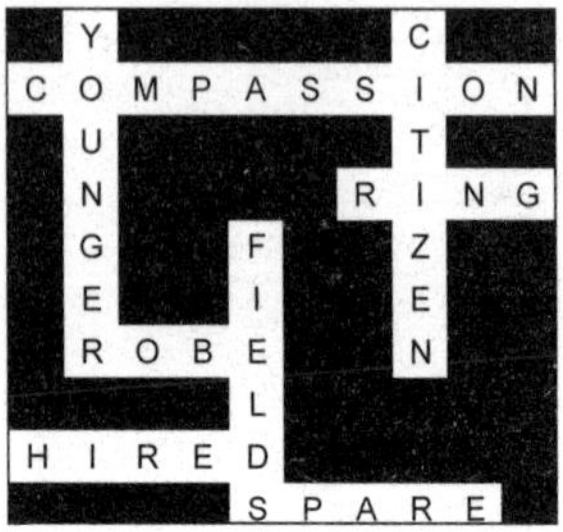
YOUNGER
CITIZEN
COMPASSION
RING
FIELD
ROBE
HIRED
SPARE

63

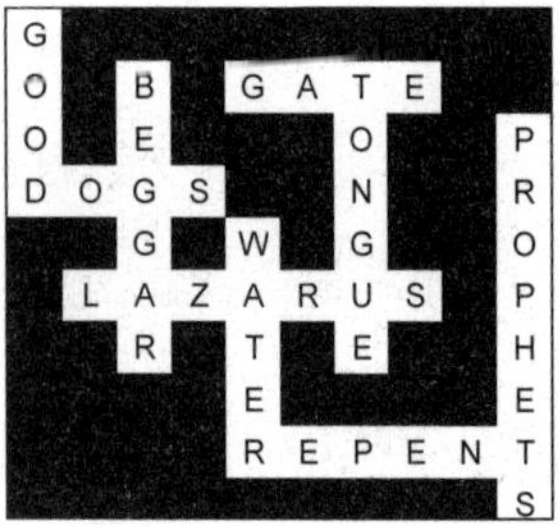
GOOD
BEGGAR
GATE
TONGUE
DOGS
PROPHETS
WATER
LAZARUS
REPENT

64

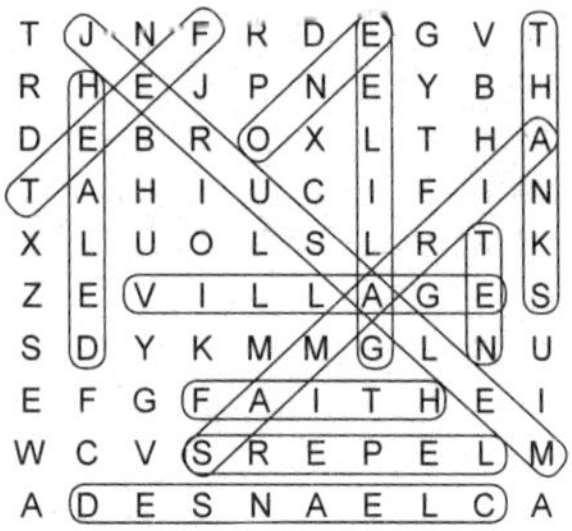
T J N F R D E G V T
R H E J P N E Y B H
D E B R O X L T H A
T A H I U C I F I N
X L U O L S L R T K
Z E V I L L A G E S
S D Y K M M G L N U
E F G F A I T H E I
W C V S R E P E L M
A D E S N A E L C A

65

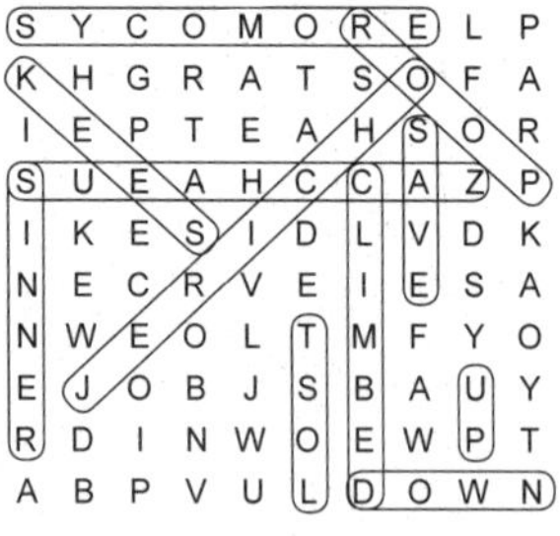
S Y C O M O R E L P
K H G R A T S O F A
I E P T E A H S O R
S U E A H C C A Z P
I K E S I D L V D K
N E C R V E I E S A
N W E O L T M F Y O
E J O B J S B A U Y
R D I N W O E W P T
A B P V U L D O W N

66

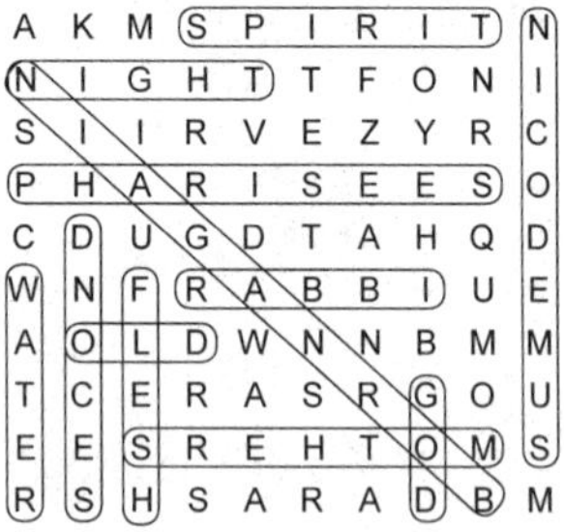
A K M S P I R I T N
N I G H T T F O N I
S I I R V E Z Y R C
P H A R I S E E S O
C D U G D T A H Q D
W N F R A B B I U E
A O L D W N N B M M
T C E R A S R G O U
E E S R E H T O M S
R S H S A R A D B M

67

```
A P H I L I P S A E
R I C B U Y T W O N
F D E D A E W H P U
R A S T K R E V E T
E E A S Y E L O T H
H R A O F I V E E A
T B Q M W M E C Y N
A X I A N D R E W K
G N U N I S I T P S
F U I Y T H E A R O
```

68

69

```
            L I F E
        T   O
W       L A Z A R U S
E       K   R
E       E
P       C A V E
I       W
N       A G A I N
G L O R Y
```

70

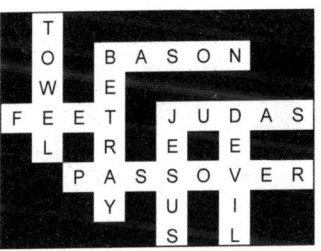

71

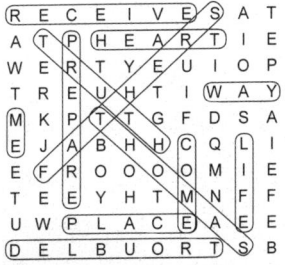

72

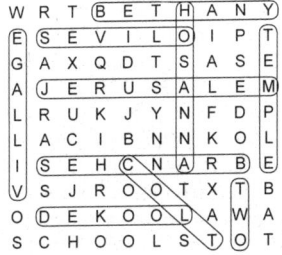

73

74

75
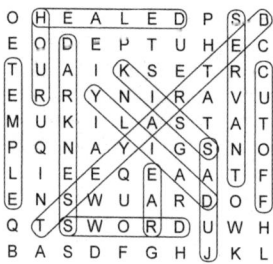

76

77
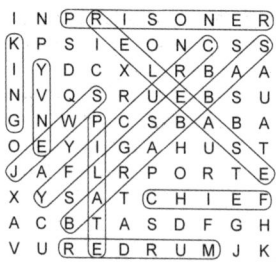

78
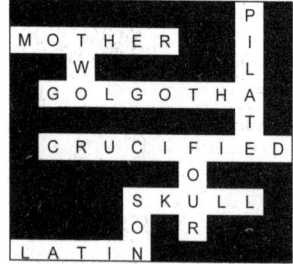

79

80
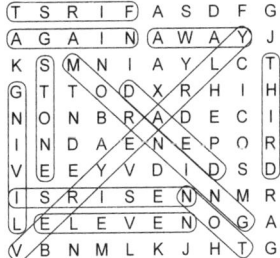

82
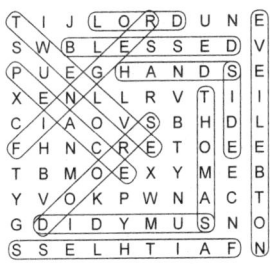

81

83

84
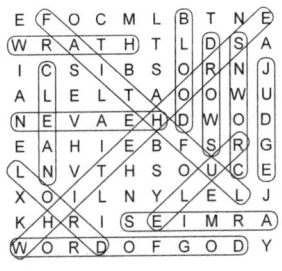

MORE BIBLE FUN!

The World's Greatest Bible Trivia for Kids

With trivia questions covering the who? the where? the what?. . .and more of scripture, you'll love this fantastic Bible knowledge-building book!

Paperback / 978-1-68322-772-4 / $4.99

Find This and More from Barbour Publishing
at Your Favorite Bookstore
or at www.barbourbooks.com